THINKING TODAY AS IF TOMORROW MATTERED

THINKING
TODAY AS IF
TOMORROW
MATTERED

The Rise of a Sustainable Consciousness

JOHN ADAMS

EARTHEART
ENTERPRISES

San Francisco, California

Published by EARTHEART ENTERPRISES
1360 4th Avenue
San Francisco, CA 94122

Publisher's Cataloging-in-Publication Data
Adams, John D., 1942 –
    Thinking today as if tomorrow mattered: the rise of a sustainable consciousness /
    / John D. Adams – San Francisco, Calif. : Eartheart Enterprises, 2000.
       p. cm.
    ISBN 0-9672859-0-9
    Includes bibliographical references.
    1. Environmental responsibility. 2. Environmental ethics. 3. Sustainable
    development. I. Title.
GE195.7 .A33   2000   99-90449
304.2   dc—21   CIP

PROJECT COORDINATION BY JENKINS GROUP, INC.

03 02 01 00 ✻ 5 4 3 2 1

Printed in the United States of America

Contents

Foreword   *vii*

Acknowledgments   *xiii*

Dedication/Introduction   *1*

SECTION I:
THE BRIGHTER THE LIGHT THE DARKER THE SHADOW

ONE   *Albert Einstein Meets Ronald Laing*   9

TWO   *Exponential Madness*   25

THREE   *The Financial System Has The*
           Tallest Buildings   33

SECTION II:
WE CAN'T RESOLVE ANY OF THESE CHALLENGES
WE CAN ONLY RESOLVE ALL OF THEM

FOUR   *Mother Nature Will Be Just Fine*   47

FIVE   *The Ever Receding Goal of Economic*
           Development   63

SIX   *Global Crowding*   81

SECTION III:
FROM AUTOPILOT TO CHOICE

SEVEN   *Somebody Ought To Do Something*
           About That   97

EIGHT   *If We Had A Mind To . . .*   105

Section IV:
Thinking Into the Future

Nine   The Hurrier I Go The Behinder I Get   129
Ten   Thinking Today as if Tomorrow Mattered   149

              References and Further Reading   169
              Order Information   173

Foreword

~

THERE ARE GROWING INDICATIONS, FROM A GREAT MANY SOURCES, THAT WITHIN
the next 30 years the human race will make an irrevocable decision
about its future on Planet Earth. I personally don't think this is in question. What I definitely think *is* questionable is whether or not this decision will be made consciously or by default. But before I go on, I want
to acknowledge that several well meaning and dedicated explorers *do
not* think that there is anything to be concerned about. Among others,
science writer Ronald Bailey (1993) of Washington, DC and University
of Maryland economics professor Julian Simon (1984) have written,
with not inconsiderable passion that there are no significant challenges arising in the environment, in the depletion of "key" resources,
in our global economy, or from continued population growth.

At the opposite end of the spectrum, there are a growing number of
people who feel equally passionately that the human race is not superior to any other species, and that any activities (e.g. economic) which
place us in a superior position are in violation of natural and/or spiritual laws. Recommendations from this contingent are most often
along the lines of restoring human life styles to those of the indigenous
people of the world.

In another sort of polarization, there are those who believe that
business, as the only institution which spans the globe, is in the best
position to initiate the changes that will be required before too much
longer to establish and maintain a just and suitable quality of human

life on the planet. Many of these people will be cited in the succeeding chapters of this book. Alternatively, there are many (e.g. Mander, 1991) who believe just as passionately that business is inherently flawed and can never respond appropriately to secure our future. This school of thought argues for extensive grass roots actions.

Nobody really knows for sure what will transpire over the next three decades. In all likelihood, there will be unexpected surprises that cause all the prognosticators to miss the mark. *My own expectation is that very serious and complex challenges will emerge, and that we can see the "seeds" of these challenges all around us today.* I may be wrong, and I won't be unhappy at all if I am wrong. But "what if" I, and the others who share my expectations, are at least partially right? By the time we are proved beyond a doubt to be right, will it be too late to address the complex systems challenges? One of my present favorite questions is *"At what point will it be too late to take a more "preventive" stance towards any unexpected, unintended or unwanted environmental or economics side effects of human activity?"* Systems dynamics become extremely complex when a great many variables are involved, and there is really no way to know for sure just when the challenges already set into motion by human activity will become irreversible.

I feel humble as I write this book, for it is addressing complex systems interactions that are far beyond anyone's understanding. But from what I have been able to understand so far, I place myself among those who think that massive changes will soon be called for in how we conduct our human activities. My own work over the past 30 years has been focused on the self-fulfilling and self-reinforcing nature of human beliefs. As a result, my conclusion is that if we are to successfully make the changes in human activities that may well be called for in the not too distant future, we will first have to change how we think about things — our values about what's important to us and our beliefs about what we need to be "successful."

To this end, I encourage you to become aware of the mindset with which you are approaching the reading of this book. If you find that you are thinking in predominantly short term and local ways; that you favor quick solutions to issues; and that you choose to fill your life with activities and possessions; you may soon conclude that this book is too alarmist and put it away without finishing it. If you find that your thinking is more regularly long term and global; that you favor getting to the core of an issue before deciding to act; and that you choose to fill your life with pursuits of "being" rather than "doing and having;" you may conclude that this book, while on the right track, doesn't go far enough or suggest sufficiently radical actions.

The mindset which I have attempted to maintain while writing this book — indeed the mindset I nowadays aspire to at all times — is one which simultaneously balances the short term with the long term; the local perspective with the global, the treatment of symptoms with the identification of the core issue; and "doing/having" with "being." This is the mindset that I will argue is needed now if we are to prepare ourselves for a future that works for everyone.

It is my hope that this book will serve as a wake-up call for its readers to what I think most people already know if they really stop to think about it — if we continue to think as we have always thought, we are likely to continue acting as we have in the past, leading to the same results we have always gotten. Every one of us is involved in co-creating whatever future we are going to experience. I am simply urging us to carry out this process of co-creation with conscious intent rather than having it arise from unconscious autopilot patterns of thinking and behaving.

I was recently surprised by a survey conducted by a professional association on its membership. The profession is one that avowedly is concerned about the future and presents itself to the public as being supportive of, even facilitative of, planned change. When this group was asked what it felt were the most important issues that they needed to address in their professional activities, most responses were about how to improve the effectiveness of their client's short term operations. *Only seven percent of the respondents suggested that longer*

range, bigger picture considerations should receive priority attention.
Not one of the hundreds of professionals who responded to the survey
suggested that a sustainable future should be a priority within their
professional practices.

This discovery was initially a surprise to me. I subsequently began
asking clients and participants in my seminars to brainstorm what
they felt were the prevailing default or automatic mindsets in their
communities and places of work. What I have found from doing this is
very revealing — especially if you can buy the idea that our mindsets
tend to be both self-fulfilling and self-reinforcing! Almost all of the
items on these brainstorming lists suggest that Western society can be
characterized as holding a short term, impatient, greedy, cynical and
superficial outlook on day to day life. Is it any wonder then, that even
a group of professionals who are avowedly concerned about the future
do not consider the future when asked about their professional priorities?

Thinking Today as if Tomorrow Mattered is organized into four sections. Section I is called "The brighter the light, the darker the shadow." It contains three chapters, which paint the backdrop for the challenges to a consciousness that is sustainable. Chapter 1 addresses our
tendencies to *not* think about *how* we think; Chapter 2 helps the reader understand the nature and impact of rates of growth; and Chapter
3 explores the question "Who *should* take responsibility for our common good?"

Section II, which is called "We can't resolve any of these challenges,
we can only resolve all of them," also contains three chapters. Each
chapter in this section explores and summarizes one of the three
"external" sets of symptoms that are receiving growing attention these
days. Chapter 4 develops the non-negotiable ecological conditions
which by scientific definition must be met if life is to continue on the
Earth; Chapter 5 addresses the challenges created by the presently
prevailing global economic system; and Chapter 6 addresses the challenges of the continuing growth of our global human population.

Section III is called "From autopilot to choice," and explores the nature of the human mindset. Chapter 7 reviews our natural tendencies to look for "somebody" (else) to hold responsible for our long term well being; Chapter 8 explores the nature of mindset and suggests ways that we can learn to think in broader, longer range terms, to increase our mental versatility and thereby increase our behavioral repertoires. Presumably, with greater mental and behavioral versatility, we will have increased our ability to create consciously an acceptable and sustainable future.

Section IV is called "Thinking into the future." Chapter 9 focuses on the individual, and provides suggestions for how each of us can sustain high level performance, health and balance during the turbulent times ahead; and Chapter 10 concludes with a look at the nature of a sustainable mind set and provides direction for encouraging the emergence of such a mind set.

Every section introduction and every chapter ends with a series of questions that are intended to be used for dialogue and for further personal contemplation. These questions were generated by a large audience of about 1500 people, who work with change professionally, in response to the challenge I gave them at the close of a keynote speech: "What questions should we be asking ourselves and what questions should we be asking our profession?" This activity was stimulated by the notion that *now is the time to identify what the appropriate questions are rather than to rush to solutions to what may turn out to be the wrong question.* Over 1000 questions were generated. These were then sorted to rule out duplications and to form themes. The few hundred final questions are included throughout the text of this book. I hope that you'll find them to be both provocative and useful.

In the final hours of her life, anthropologist Margaret Mead had a vision that she shared with her friend and former student, Jean Houston. Her vision was for the survival of the world, which she saw happening through the establishment of teaching-learning communities in which people gathered in small groups on a regular basis in homes, schools, churches, and businesses. She saw these people in dialogue, taking their learning and conclusions into social action.[1] Hopefully, these question sets will foster group dialogues of the sort Margaret Mead envisioned. The first few questions follow. Reflect on your own answers. They have also proven to be wonderful for guiding group dialogues.

QUESTIONS FOR CONTEMPLATION AND DIALOGUE

- ✧ Can the dissemination of information about emerging global conditions sensitize enough people? Can such dissemination provide a wake-up call?

- ✧ What mindset changes am I ready and willing to undertake in my own life?

- ✧ What am I going to start doing differently right now?

---

[1] Jean Houston. "Dear Mr. President: Ask the Great Questions" in *The Noetic Sciences Review.* The Institute of Noetic Sciences, Sausalito, CA, Spring 1997, pp 37-38.

Acknowledgments

I FIRST BECAME INTERESTED IN HOW THE FUTURE UNFOLDS IN GRADUATE SCHOOL during the second half of the 60's. After completing two degrees in mathematics, I decided to change to the study of Organizational Behavior, partly because I learned that the process of actually implementing changes (such as mathematical models for how often to hire flight attendants when training time and turnover are known) was much more challenging than developing the mathematical models that might help a system to function more effectively.

On my first day in graduate school, I had the opportunity to visit Herb Shepard, who was the founder and Chairman of the Organizational Behavior group at (then) Case Institute of Technology, in his office. On the blackboard was an exponential curve that, from left to right, rose up the blackboard very slowly at first; then it turned the corner and shot straight up. In my earlier math studies I had been intrigued with how steady growth rates cause this exponential curve phenomenon, so I commented that the drawing on the blackboard made me feel right at home. Herb chuckled and said that he had just concluded a seminar in which advanced students and he had been exploring the implications of world population growth on business life and practice in the future. This was 1965, and the population on the planet was just over three billion (just about half of what we have today, only 30 years later!). Herb mentioned that they had become quite alarmed at the idea that we would have five billion people alive

xiii

at the same time by 1990, if the exponential curve didn't "tip over" for some reason in the next 25 years.

Another professor, Newton Margulies, came into the room and joined the conversation, pointing out that one of our challenges eventually would be to take seriously the implications of growth, and of the parallel rates of depletion that would come along with growth. None of the three of us knew it at the time, but that casual conversation was to have a profound impact on my life and work!

A few years later, sometime in the early '70's, I watched a PBS documentary on the rate of our consumption of fossil fuels. At the time my father was working in the natural gas industry, and we also had many conversations about how soon we might run out of fuel reserves. As if to add emphasis to this growing concern of mine, the 1973 oil crisis occurred, giving me many hours of sitting in lines at gas stations to ponder on the future of humanity if its fuel consumption patterns didn't change. These coinciding events left an indelible impression on my consciousness. I was left with the question of "How do we make society-wide changes?"

Little did I know at the time, but the seeds of my own conclusions about what it would take to shift mindsets all across the world had already been planted. My dissertation, completed in 1969, was called *Phases of Personal and Professional Development*, and was about the predictable aspects of personal development in a professional development program. After completing my studies, I journeyed to The University of Leeds to teach in the Management Studies Department. Within two weeks of my arrival in the U.K., I was sent by the Chairman of my department to conduct a seminar at a remote location on the North Sea coast. It was there that I would meet Barrie Hopson, who at the time was Director of the Vocational Guidance Research Unit back at the University of Leeds.

Since the weather was cold and wet, we all spent a lot of time by the fireplace, and Barrie and I soon became fast friends. I quickly learned that he had also just recently completed his graduate studies, and that his interest was career development. In the course of our mutual sharing, we discovered that the conclusions he had reached in his dissertation were much the same as those I had reached in mine. Shortly after returning home to Leeds, we concluded that our common discoveries pointed to a generic model of adjustment to personal changes such as divorce, job change, bereavement, and so on. Another faculty member in Management Studies, John Hayes, excitedly pointed out that he, too, had reached the same conclusions in his own studies. The three of us decided to write a book about a generic model of personal transition (Adams, Hayes, and Hopson, 1976).

The discipline of writing that first book caused me to reflect on my previous writing focuses — papers in graduate school and a few articles — and I discovered that I had always written essentially the "same" paper — everything was about individual effectiveness at work.

This focus continued when I was asked by Jan Margolis, then Director of Human Resources at a large community hospital in Washington, DC, to prepare a three hour introduction to stress management, based on the chapters on stress I had written for *Transition*. That introduction, in June of 1975, was so successful that I was asked to spend the next two and a half years on retainer to the hospital to further develop my interests in transition and stress.

As my work on stress management unfolded over the succeeding years, I began to focus on the centrality of personal beliefs in the experience of stress. My learning in this area eventually led to my interests in human consciousness and the role of the "self fulfilling prophecy" in everyday life — that what one holds in one's consciousness is what one tends to find in his or her experience of life. From this point onwards, not only has my work been focused on individual effectiveness in the workplace, but also on the role of human consciousness in every aspect of human effectiveness. I must acknowledge the many thousands of participants in my workshops for gradually teaching me about this important facet of my work. *Real transformation occurs one mindset at a time!*

From 1985 until 1992 I worked in partnership with Sabina Spencer. We spent many hours musing over human consciousness and inventing ways to raise people's awareness of *how* we think. We used our seminar, *The Strategic Leadership Perspective*, to test and validate our ideas.

The final step in my journey towards sustainable consciousness happened in the late autumn of 1991, when Willis Harman, a founding board member of The World Business Academy, asked me to chair a task force on the role of business in a sustainable future. I accepted the request without thinking about it much, and started recruiting task force members. Soon a group of WBA members were meeting regularly to explore the next 30 years and to define what stake business might have in determining, consciously or unconsciously, what the world of 2022 might look like. As we continued to work with the concept of 30 years, I came to realize that my newborn grandson, Jonathan, would also reach 30, and be in the prime of his life, at about the same time.

As this sank in, my interest in "sustainable development" shifted from urgent to passionate! My question became one of "Whose future is it anyway?" Would the eventual outcomes of the activities of my generation be at the expense of Jonathan's generation, or would we find a way to pass on a worthwhile "inheritance?"

The work of our task force also made clear to me that a sustainable future is about more than cleaning up the environment. I soon concluded that we must consider at least the global environment (molecular trash, whether waterborne or airborne, is no respecter of national boundaries); the global economy (which requires continuous quantitative growth to sustain its present form); the global population (which continues to grow largely unchecked in those areas that are most economically destitute); and human consciousness (which in most of us either ignores the environment, economic viability, and rampant population growth, or wishes that "somebody" would do "something" about those awful situations). If we address only one of these dimensions we can only treat symptoms. I believe that our only route to a quality future is to address them all, both systemically and systematically.

I am especially grateful to my colleague and dear friend, Ralph Copleman, for his continuous encouragement and for his support, both tangible and intangible, in getting *Thinking Today as if Tomorrow Mattered* into book form. Ralph's reading of the near final manuscript lead to many small changes that make the message clearer.

I must also express my eternal gratitude to my wife, Rhoda Nussbaum, for her continuous support, patience, encouragement, and, in the early days of my work on this manuscript, for providing a "hideaway" where I could work away from the distractions of the everyday world. Her gentle pressure to get this book out was invaluable.

Dedication and Introduction:

To the Next Generation

~

I FIRST BECAME ACTIVELY INVOLVED IN THE EXPLORATION OF WHAT IT WILL TAKE to establish a high quality, sustainable future around the planet during the late Autumn of 1991, when I was invited by the World Business Academy to chair a task force. Our assignment was to look into the potential role of business around the world in establishing and protecting an acceptable and maintainable quality of life for everyone (now six billion and still growing!). I immediately said "yes," but I didn't grasp how passionately I would become involved for a few days.

I flew to Washington to visit my older daughter Samantha, and to meet my first grandson for the first time! He had just turned three months old.

"Of course!" I thought. "This sustainability work isn't so much about me and my interests as it is about Jonathan and his interests!" We had adopted a thirty year time frame in our sustainability task force. As I flew all the way across the country to make this young man's acquaintance, I reflected on what life would be like in thirty years if we all continued to operate as we have been operating, and if we all continue to worship short term economic health as our "deity in use." By the time I got to Washington, I was hooked. "The Future" had transformed itself in my soul from being an avocation to becoming my primary life's work. Most of all, this book is dedicated to Jonathan's future.

I want to make this dedication into an introductory portion of the book by sharing the statements made by two groups of young people. One is a group of elementary school children from Berkeley, California. The second is a group of teenagers who formed a "Youth Summit" at the UN sponsored Earth Conference held in Rio in June of 1992.

The first group is made up of a classroom in a school in Berkeley, California. The theme for the school year for this group of third and fourth graders was the environment. This means that they did their reading lessons, geography lessons, arithmetic lessons, and so on, through the "lens" of the global environment. I was introduced to this group by a graduate student who had taken a class from me and shared my interest in our future. When I mentioned to the class I was teaching that I had been asked to deliver a keynote speech on the next thirty years at a national convention, and that I would really like to get some kids involved, one of the class members said that a friend of his was a teacher's aide at an elementary school in Berkeley where the environment was a central theme for the coming school year.

Within a very short period of time, my graduate student had made contact with the third and fourth grade class, and reported back to me that they were interested in helping me with my presentation!

A few days later, I went to meet the class, and within minutes of my arrival, found myself sitting on the floor with them, playing and enjoying myself. My own excitement rose as I noticed how diverse the group of 18 youngsters was — there were Caucasians, African-Americans, Japanese, Chinese, Hispanics, Israelis, and Moslems. My excitement was that these kids represented virtually the whole world! I introduced myself and told the young people what my speech was going to be about. Many of them nodded wisely as I described my message. I told them that what I wanted from them was a brief statement from each person about what they wanted the world to be like thirty years from now, when they would be the age of most of the people sitting in the audience. I stayed for a while longer, hoping that they'd become comfortable enough with me that my presence on the podium would be sufficient to give them the courage to stand up in front of 1500 people, one at a time, and deliver their statements.

Ten days later, when they marched into the grand ballroom of the downtown convention hotel, every head in the audience turned to look, and a surprised and excited buzz filled the ballroom. This group had never had children invited into their midst before, and the anticipation of what would happen next was palpable!

When it came time for the children to make their statements, three quarters of the way through my speech, they each strode confidently to the microphone and boomed out the following statements about their hopes and fears for 30 years from now:

- ◇ "I see flowers, more streams and rivers, and a lot more wildlife. The ozone layer is fixed and there are a lot more animals."
- ◇ "I want to walk up Telegraph Avenue and see no homeless people. I don't ever want to see any homeless people again!"
- ◇ "I just wish people weren't so greedy!"
- ◇ "I want people to just buy what they need and compost and recycle what is left over."
- ◇ "I want there to be solar powered cars and solar heated stadiums so people can play baseball year 'round."
- ◇ "I want the school buses to have smog checks. And I want the wolves to not be killed, because they'll soon be extinct if they're killed."
- ◇ "If there are any homeless people, I want them to have better shelters and enough food."
- ◇ "I want there to be more solar powered cars and less gas stations."
- ◇ "I want there to be no more endangered species, and that people won't just kill animals for fun. People should treat animals like themselves — if they have guns they can shoot targets instead of living things."

✧ "If there are fishing industries, I hope they'll spare the dolphins and the whales — I wish they'd start right now!"

✧ "I hope the oceans and the seas and the whole world aren't polluted, and endangered species won't be killed, and there won't be any wars."

✧ "I want people to treat animals more like humans, because there's not a big difference between humans and animals."

✧ "I hope there is no money and that people can get food and necessities whenever they need to."

✧ "I want people to be using more clay plates and bowls and cups instead of Styrofoam because it's bad for the ozone. I also wish a woman could be president."

✧ "I wish the homeless could all have jobs and that the streets would not be dirty."

✧ I hope that things won't cost too much so people can buy what they need.

✧ "I hope all the grizzly bears won't be killed, and I wish that people would take more responsibility and think before they do stuff like killing animals."

✧ "I want the oceans and lakes and streams to have less pollution."

The second group was made up of teenagers from all over the world who attended the Earth Summit in Rio de Janeiro, Brazil in June of 1992. Their gathering was called The First Global Youth Summit. These young men and women symbolically represented the "stakeholders for the future" at the Earth Summit. In fact, one of them states very proudly "We *are* the future!" The statements that follow are taken from a videotape of their gathering.

✧ "It takes a drop to start a waterfall, and the waterfall will come from us." (Trinidad)

✧ "Just keep shouting as hard as you can and as high as you can." (Africa)

✧ "When you come together with people from all around the

world, and you are all fighting for the same thing, we have strength together; not just when you stand alone; you say there is hope. WE ARE the hope! That's why I'm here!" (African American)

✧ "I am here because I want to believe there is something I can do. I want to know that there are other people like me who want to get rid of prejudice, and who want to see and believe that there are different kinds of people, and get over stereotypes of different countries." (Indonesia)

✧ "However small it is what we do in our home communities, that somewhere in Sweden, that somewhere in Japan, that somewhere in New Zealand, someone is doing the same thing — and with the same energy and the same hope!" (Sweden)

✧ "One of the things I read once was that we weren't really endangering the Earth. The Earth has survived for millennia, through millions of years of changes and evolution. What we have to save is ourselves." (U.S.A.)

✧ "What do you see for the future? What can you do for the future? What's your vision? What's your wish?" (U.S.A.)

✧ "Nobody has any right answers, all we can do is try, try, try". (U.S.A.)

✧ "We are here exploring our values — what it means to be a leader and a group member, what it means to empower each other. We're here to become global citizens; to create a youth agenda full of action steps we can take to make a difference in the world." (U.S.A.)

✧ "The more they hear us and see us, the more they will make decisions remembering that this is our future they're talking about.." (African American)

✧ "After we've spoken and thought, we have to get up and do. Dear friends, we are not just leaders of the future, we are the leaders of today! We are the role models for generations to come." (African American)

✧ "I don't know if this is the first time, but it's at least the first time in a long time that I've felt hopeful". (U.S.A.)

And so I want to dedicate this book to my grandson, Jonathan, to all of the children quoted above, and to all the rest of the children (of all ages) who are our hope for the future. In making this dedication, it is my fervent hope that we will come to see the next generations as the receivers of a legacy of thoughtfulness rather than as those who will have to clean up after us and learn to live with less than we have lived with.

QUESTIONS FOR CONTEMPLATION AND DIALOGUE

- ✧ To whom in the next generation shall I dedicate my work?
- ✧ How can we involve children more as stakeholders for the future in our work?
- ✧ How can we more fully appreciate all generations?
- ✧ If I expect to be around in 30 years, what contributions can I make now that I'll look back on with pride?
- ✧ How shall we embody the children's message — what do we do first to deliver a sustainable future to them?
- ✧ How can we involve young people in the design and implementation of global action plans?

SECTION I

The Brighter the Light
The Darker the Shadow

As I mentioned in the foreword, I frequently begin my classes and seminars by asking the people with me to brainstorm what they consider to be the most widely shared characteristics of the prevailing mindset in the Western world today. I invariably find the list to be dominated by items like the following:

Short sighted	Sound bites
Greedy	Violence oriented
Superficial	Soap operas
Look out for #1	Materialistic
Busy/Rushed	Do more with less
Quick fix	Intolerant
Faster/bigger is better	The board won't let me
Continuous growth	If it ain't broke, don't fix it
Market share/profit/bottom line	

I then ask them to reflect on what their scenarios of the future are if we continue to reflect these qualities in our shared way of thinking. Extrapolating qualities such as these into an ever more unpredictable future (are these very qualities not the ones that make the future less and less predictable?) always leads to pretty gloomy scenarios.

I think it's also appropriate to ask what we can expect from our work or our professions if we do an impeccable job and are completely successful, *while operating from mindsets such as these.* If someone's daily efforts are based on short cycles, and working ever faster to do more with less, is not that person's effort primarily going to add pressure to our growing system of challenges? This is the reason for the title of this section — the "brighter" our work, when carried out from the prevailing mindset, the "darker" the results when viewed from a bigger picture, longer time frame perspective!

Questions For Contemplation and Dialogue

✧ How can we keep up the personal commitment to change when it seems to take so much energy?

✧ What are the long term implications of what I do each day?

✧ What do I want the world to be like in 30 years and what will I do to contribute to that outcome?

✧ In what ways do we all collude with an unsustainable system? How are we each perpetuating the status quo?

✧ What difference could I make anyhow?

✧ What are the "right things to do" to foster a sustainable consciousness?

✧ Are people in my line of work part of the problem or part of the solution?

✧ Is my work more about generating money in the short term or adding value in the long term?

✧ How can I and my colleagues/work mates model new ways of being?

✧ What will people in my line of work have to let go of to make the changes that seem to be called for?

✧ What other organizations or professions can mine form alliances with to establish broader perspectives?

✧ What will it take to get a critical mass to engage in exploring questions such as these?

ONE

Albert Einstein Meets Ronald Laing

"A new idea is first condemned as ridiculous, then dismissed as trivial; until finally it becomes what everyone knows."

WILLIAM JAMES

"It must be remembered that there is nothing more difficult to plan, more doubtful of success, nor more dangerous to manage than the creation of a new system. For the initiator has the enmity of all who profit by the preservation of the old institutions and merely lukewarm defenders in those who might gain by the new."

MACHIAVELLI — TO THE PRINCE

I would feel that Albert Einstein's statement that:

'We cannot expect to be able to resolve any complex problems from within the same state of consciousness that created them.'

is incredibly overused, especially in the recent literature describing the ecological challenges we may soon be facing, if there were strong indications that a critical mass of people were in fact moving rapidly towards a "larger" or broader state of consciousness. My experience is that instead of shifting our consciousness, most of us are trying harder and harder to make our old familiar approaches work, with progressively poorer outcomes and ever-increasing levels of daily stress as a result.

The reason for this, I think, lies in a much less frequently cited statement made by the late Scottish psychiatrist, Ronald Laing (1990). In his view:

> *"The range of what we think and do is limited by what we **fail** to notice. And **because** we fail to notice **that** we fail to notice, there is little we can do to change, **until** we notice how failing to notice shapes our thoughts and deeds."*

What I want to emphasize by putting Einstein and Laing into juxtaposition is the idea that we may have the option of changing our consciousness only if we first become more cognizant of the qualities and effects of the consciousness which is prevalent today. I suggested in the introduction to this section that the prevailing consciousness, across much of the world, seems to be one that is short term, narrow and superficial, greedy and self centered, and "activity" oriented. If this is more or less true, on a broad scale, and if our thoughts do indeed influence our actions and thereby the results we get, then is it any wonder that so many people are feeling more stressed out than they ever have in the past and that so many of our institutions don't seem to be working any more?

Our challenge then, according to Laing, is first to become more conscious of *how* we are presently thinking about those things that really matter in our lives, and *then* to be aware of any changes in our mindsets which we conclude would be appropriate. Then maybe we won't have to be reminded of Einstein's statement anymore!

How many of us could have accurately predicted our personal situations today if we had tried to do so 10 years ago? Not many, I dare say. There are just too many "surprises" that occur, like "wild cards" in a poker game, for prognostications to be very accurate. And yet, short of natural disasters, most of those wild cards, if we think about them, are "played" by others who are making conscious choices in their own self interest. In hindsight, we can often recognize that the seeds of the unexpected occurrences were there all along, but we didn't attend to them.

As an example, a few people discovered in the middle 1980s that a lot of money could be made quickly through leveraged buy outs (short term, greedy, self centered), and soon LBOs were all the rage, wreaking havoc on the lives of tens of thousands of formerly loyal employees and their families.

And a growing number of natural scientists are even concluding that many of the natural disasters, such as floods and droughts, are also created by human activity. The manufacture of a product always creates a certain amount of waste and a certain amount of effluent which are released into the environment. Even driving a car releases several pounds of carbon dioxide into the atmosphere for every tank of fuel. Those scientists (probably over 90% of the total) who subscribe to the idea that there are global warming gasses are today suggesting that these industrial and automotive effluents, which may cause wide scale global warming in the not too distant future, are also at least partly responsible for many of the unusual extremes in weather that are occurring (flooding, droughts, hurricanes, etc.) with more and more frequency these days. But most of the time, most of us pay little conscious attention to the possible connection between human activities and those changing weather patterns.

In 1993, a book was published called *Today, Then* (Walter, 1993), which contains a fascinating account of predictions made for the 1893 World's Columbian Exposition held in Chicago about what life in the USA would be like 100 years hence, in 1993. Many of the leading academics and business leaders of the day, including George Westinghouse, W.R. Grace, William Jennings Bryant, plus several members of President Benjamin Harrison's cabinet, submitted their predictions. When these predictions came to light a few years ago, a man named Dave Walter was so astounded at how *inaccurate* most of the predictions were that he decided to edit and publish them, as an example of how difficult accurate prognostication is.

Among the predictions that turned out to be accurate were:

◇ the advent of an income tax,

◇ air conditioning for homes,

◇ women permitted to vote,

◇ Florida would boom as a leisure state,

◇ cities would become "groups of suburbs,"

◇ telephones and telegraphs would be used for urgent communications.

Telephones were predicted to become so important that there would be one in every city!

Among the far longer and more crucial list of *inaccurate* predictions were:

◇ cities would be built of aluminum,

◇ unemployment would disappear,

◇ railroads would be the fastest mode of travel,

◇ hot air balloons would be prevalent as a form of air travel,

◇ mail would still be delivered by stagecoach and horseback,

◇ everyone would enjoy a three hour workday,

◇ simplified laws would bring an end to the legal profession,

◇ 120 year life expectancy,

◇ war would be nonexistent,

◇ mankind would control nature.

There was no mention of the communications and home entertainment possibilities created by the electronics breakthroughs of the second half of the 20th century.

Walter suggests that the main reasons for inaccuracies in forecasting the future are first that inventions are constantly taking place which we don't know about (e.g. the 1893 forecasters were unaware of the motorcar advances underway in Germany). Secondly, we tend to be so dominated by our recent pasts that we are likely to make predictions about the future based on recent developments rather than possible future breakthroughs. The same influences are surely present today in our homes and workplaces.

Why is it that people's best efforts to create visions and strategic plans in business are so often frustrated? Even seemingly obvious efforts to improve people's work productivity most often become "flavor of the month," as has frequently been the case over the past 10 years or so with quality programs and reengineering efforts. Further, those who have been on work team retreats will probably recognize how the plans generated during those activities seem to fade away when the team members return to their "real world" and face the pressures that have built up while they were away on the retreat.

Much of the time, managers seem to be forced to practice "first aid" management, scurrying to fix minor problems and correct small deviations, with little encouragement to operate in ways that would foster a more strategic perspective. Ten o'clock deadlines always seem to drive out the longer-range plans.

Now we are seeing a similar stalling momentum in the vision creation activities carried out by a rapidly growing number of organizations around the globe. The leader involves people in articulating a vision for the enterprise, and soon becomes frustrated by the lack of any abiding alteration in performance. Too often, the "transformational" breakthroughs fail to materialize, and the legions of "aligned" and "empowered" organizational members don't emerge. Small wonder that vision work often generates only cynicism.

As Ronald Laing accurately pointed out, in these instances when improvement programs fail and visions rapidly fade, we fail to notice that the prevailing "autopilot" mindsets are looking, on a very localized level, for short term benefits. Our performance appraisal and reward systems, which reflect this prevailing outlook, continue to reinforce short-term maintenance of the status quo. The result is that those who were fostering visions and strategic plans are frustrated and don't understand why the strategic concerns and possibilities end up taking a back seat to immediate pressures.

Ingrained Habits Die Hard

As a clue to why these things happen, consider the way most of us learned to think. During the most impressionable years up to about age 12, children most often hear repeated messages from their parents and teachers about what they should never do or should stop doing. Most youngsters hear lots of messages about the mistakes they are making everyday. "Stop doing this." "Good children don't do that." "That's a pretty painting, but shouldn't the car have wheels?" Few children are told with the same regularity how bright or creative they are as they grow up.

The not so surprising result is that normal modes of thinking focus on the avoidance of mistakes, solving problems as quickly as possible, and being "response-able." Since as children, we learned to focus energy on the present, as adults we almost always allow the "10:00 o'clock deadline" to take precedence over our longer range plans. Having learned that we must defer to external structures and authorities, we continue to do just that — subconsciously. Socialized human beings don't have to stop and think about how to respond to situations, they "just do it." This is perfectly normal, and often our responses are appropriate.

And here's the challenge: the often repeated "do as you're told" of childhood, continuing to operate subconsciously in adulthood, can stifle initiative, creativity and longer range/bigger picture possibilities.

Short Term Thinking Reinforces The Status Quo

Short term, reactive, and externally focused modes of thinking reinforce the status quo. Developmental or vision-creating activities, on the other hand, demand a state of consciousness which is creative, long term, and internally driven. Since this "altered state of consciousness" is rarely reinforced in children, as adults most of us must choose it consciously or slip back quickly from vision or development supporting modes of thought to status quo supporting modes of thought.

Work structures, by their very nature, reinforce status quo thinking and behaviors and resist the opposite. Most developmental and vision creation work is doomed to short term impact at best unless a critical mass of people learn to step into the "altered states of consciousness" more frequently, and for longer periods.

Nearly all of us depend on the dominant or prevailing social system for our livelihood and our security, so there is certainly an understandable anxiety about changing it, as well as about being the first in our neighborhoods to make significant changes in how we live. For example, if my life's dream has been to have a nice car, and if my flexible working hours differ from my neighbors, then owning an economical car or car pooling to work won't seem to be very attractive to me.

It should be pretty clear that whatever future we do have over the next 20 to 30 years is likely to be strongly influenced, both directly and indirectly, by the economic and technological systems we have all participated in creating and building.

Today, it is widely held that *all* of our major challenges can be resolved by continued economic (i.e. quantitative) growth and/or the use of technology. These viewpoints are reinforced by educational processes which are, by and large, still turning out specialists who know little beyond their disciplinary boundaries and show little interest in questions that arise from beyond their areas of study.

In sum, there is little everyday pressure on us to change how we are living, and lots of reinforcement to continue along the paths we have been following. There are few, if any, processes or structures in place for guiding and supporting the degree of personal transformation that many are saying will be necessary if high quality human life is to be possible for future generations. If those who believe we are heading for trouble in the very near future are correct, then the longer we wait to take corrective action, the lower the sustainable level of quality of life will be. Once again, the underlying questions of this book are *"Will it ever be appropriate to take a more preventive stance towards the potential challenges from the environment arising from human activity?"* and *"If the answer is 'yes,' then when is our last chance to take that stance?"*

On Noticing That We Are Failing To Notice!

One way to practice a broader way of thinking is to practice moving consciously from one mode of thinking to another through asking questions that can only be answered from a particular perspective, such as "What do you think will happen if this trend continues?" or "What would you create if you had a magic wand?" While clearly an overly simplified idea, the following figure provides a vehicle for framing these consciousness shifting practice questions.

As an example, consider the **Time/Focus** matrix in Figure 1.[2] Along the **Time** dimension, the "Operational Outlook" focuses on immediate concerns, short-range implications, and rapid responses. It emphasizes analysis, correction of deviations, and consistency. This is the most widely shared and automatic (i.e. socialized) perspective, at least in the Western world.

The "Strategic Outlook," on the other hand, focuses on future outcomes, long range implications, and leadership. It emphasizes catalyzing change, prevention of problems, and the establishment of new directions. For most of us, this perspective must be consciously adopted, and can only be held for as long as we consciously choose it.

On the **Focus** dimension, the "Reactive, Outer" focus responds to external stimuli, authorities, and constraints. It emphasizes responsiveness, logic, and reaching agreement. This is the most widely shared and automatic (i.e. socialized) perspective.

The "Creative, Inner" focus arises from internal ideas and personal preferences and standards. It emphasizes initiative taking, intuition,

---

[2] An earlier version of this grid, called the "Styles of Thinking" grid, was developed by John Adams and Sabina Spencer.

Figure 1 — The Thinking Styles Grid

A T T E N T I O N F O C U S		TIME ORIENTATION	
		OPERATIONAL	STRATEGIC
	OUTER/REACTIVE	FOCUS: Immediate Problem FUNCTION: Administration LIABILITY: No Big Picture	FOCUS: Anticipation FUNCTION: Strategy Development LIABILITY: Overlook Immediate
	INNER/CREATIVE	FOCUS: New Approach FUNCTION: Innovation LIABILITY: Duplication Of Effort	FOCUS: What We Want FUNCTION: Define The Future LIABILITY: No Reality Testing

and building commitment. For most of us, this mode of thinking must be consciously adopted, and can only be held for as long as we consciously choose it.

Look again at Figure 1. The normal-socialized "Operational/Reactive" mode of thinking (upper left cell) is useful and necessary for sound administration — running a business on a day to day basis for example. It will serve the business leaders relatively well, so long as no major changes are called for. But if it is relied upon solely, especially when the external environment of the business is changing rapidly and unpredictably, significant change will be very difficult to carry through. With external turbulence, the "Operational/Reactive" perspective fosters symptom management and continual fire fighting.

During the past several years, many leaders in all kinds of enterprises around the world have devoted a great deal of energy to the Strategic/Creative mode of thinking (lower right cell), which is neces-

sary for working with concepts like vision, mission, and higher purpose. It cannot be relied on solely for day to day management however, so the normal tendency to revert to the "Operational/Reactive"
mode takes over, and the visionary ideas get lost. Each of the four
modes of thinking represented in Figure 1 has its time and place, and
over-reliance on any one of them can cause difficulties and limita-
tions.

QUESTIONS FOR MENTAL FLEXIBILITY. I am not advocating that we
stop thinking in short term and reactive ways. But I do think that we
need to expand the "zones of comfort" in the ways we think. For most
us, our "autopilot," or default, ways of thinking reflect rather narrow
zones of comfort and we "fail to notice" that we are so narrow. The
"Thinking Styles" grid is a convenient way to help us begin to notice
that we are failing to notice, and it also can guide us in forming the
questions that will broaden our mental zones of comfort.

Each of the four cells in the grid in Figure 1 requires a different state
of consciousness. The questions which follow automatically take you
to the different cells. The regular asking and answering of these questions gradually expands your zone of comfort in thinking. One aspect
of effective leaders is that they automatically ask themselves questions
such as these all the time.

1. *Operational Reactive:* What are the immediate needs of the sit-
    uation? What needs attention right now?

2. *Strategic Reactive:* What do I expect to happen if things contin-
    ue as they are? What trends should we be tracking?

3. *Operational Creative:* Is there a different way I can approach this
    situation? What new interpretation can we come up with?

4. *Strategic Creative:* How would I change this situation if I had a
    magic wand? If we knew we could not fail, what would we do?

Each of us will most easily and naturally ask questions from our
most comfortable cell and tend naturally to overlook the questions
from our least comfortable cell.

Whenever we find ourselves resisting a change or feel that we are spinning our wheels, questions such as these can lead to break-throughs, or at least progress. Each of us will have a favored quadrant which we "think from" unconsciously most of the time. Any consciousness shifts out of that favored quadrant is unlikely unless we make a conscious choice to do so — or are faced with questions like those above, which force a shift in consciousness.

As another example along these same lines, consider the **Behavioral Styles** grid in Figure 2.[3] While the grid described above (Figure 1) describes alternative ways of *thinking*, this grid describes alternative *behavioral* preferences.

Along the **Results Urgency** dimension, the "Deliberate" first column focuses on being somewhat cautious or judicious in how one approaches a given situation. It emphasizes being careful and thorough in activities, and may wait for directions about how to proceed.

Figure 2 — Behavioral Styles Grid

		RESULTS URGENCY	
E		DELIBERATE	IMPULSIVE
M		FOCUS:	FOCUS:
O		Accuracy	Urgency
	CONTROLLED	FUNCTION:	FUNCTION:
T		Analysis	Action
		LIABILITY:	LIABILITY:
I		Nitpicking	Blaming
O		FOCUS:	FOCUS:
		Relationship	Possibility
N	EXPRESSIVE	FUNCTION:	FUNCTION:
		Cooperation	Vision
S		LIABILITY:	LIABILITY:
		Conflict Avoidance	Overlook Detail

[3] This grid is adapted from an earlier version, called "Social Styles," developed by Denver psychologists Merrill and Reid. The Social Styles grid was subsequently popularized by Wilson Learning in their "Managing Interpersonal Relationships" Course.

This focus may sometimes take a long time to reach a decision, but it is unlikely that important details will be overlooked. A common statement coming from this focus is "Get it right the first time."

The "Impulsive" second column, on the other hand, focuses on taking quick action. It emphasizes efficiency and directness, and prefers to give directions or make them up rather than waiting for someone to provide them. This focus moves to action very quickly, and thereby may sometimes overlook important information or details. A common statement coming from this focus is "Get it done on time."

On the **Emotional Expression** dimension, the "Controlled" top row emphasizes rational approaches to situations, an air of formality and a clarity about expected outcomes. As a result, this focus tends to withhold personal information and feelings, preferring cool logic instead. A common statement coming from this focus is "Let's keep personalities out of this."

The "Expressive" bottom row emphasizes the importance of emotions in reaching sound conclusions, an air of informality, and attention to the people involved in a situation. Communications are effective, and people are kept up to date. This focus may get sidetracked from too much small talk. A common statement coming from this focus is "How does everyone feel about the direction we're headed?"

Look again at Figure 2. In most businesses today, the "Controlled" row of the **Emotional Expression** dimension is most highly valued. In high technology businesses, for example, this controlled emotional expression is most often coupled with the "Deliberate" column of the **Results Urgency** dimension in the engineering areas of the company. At the senior management level of these businesses, however, the "Impulsive," or high urgency column is most favored. Therefore, in order to keep up with the endless deadlines and the demands for reduced cycle times, the more naturally deliberate engineering dominated functions are today frequently found to be working longer and longer hours just to keep up with the demands for ever shorter cycle times and from the high urgency marketplace.

What often happens in companies that strongly favor the "Controlled" and "Impulsive" dimensions is that relatively few people who naturally favor the "Expressive" end of the **Emotional Expression** dimension are attracted. Thus, the focuses and functions that these people naturally bring are under represented, causing the company to be less effective overall. As a result, what often turns out to be missing, in today's fast paced businesses, are the focuses on relationships, teamwork, and new possibilities. There is also much less attention given to cooperation and vision building, in spite of the lip service that these qualities receive and the thousands of pages that are published about their importance every year.

As I pointed out in describing the Thinking Styles grid (Figure 1), when a particular cell is over used, its liabilities become more apparent. And, in truth, we find that the liabilities of overuse of the "Deliberate-Controlled" cell in Figure 2 (nitpicking and analysis-paralysis); and the "Impulsive-Controlled" cell (blaming and demanding) are rampant in most work settings today. Once again, when we "fail to notice that we fail to notice," there is a tendency to try even harder with the processes and techniques that have not been getting us the results we really want, rather than adopting another (in this case, more emotionally expressive) approach.

To be fair, a growing number of business leaders are realizing the shortcomings of the predominant emotionally controlled autopilot response in a rapidly changing, rapidly "shrinking" world. As a result, the natural talents of the more emotionally expressive behaviors, such as creating empowering climates and building compelling visions, are increasingly being sought out and rewarded.

QUESTIONS FOR BEHAVIORAL FLEXIBILITY. I am not advocating that we stop operating in emotionally controlled ways if the situation truly calls for accuracy or urgency. But I am convinced that we need to expand our "zones of comfort" in the ways we behave in our work settings, if we are to have any hope of developing sustainable working environments, and indeed sustainable economies.

For most us, our "autopilot," or default, ways of behaving reflect rather narrow zones of comfort and we "fail to notice" that we are operating in such a narrow manner. The ideas behind these two 2x2 matrices provide a convenient way to help us begin to notice that we are failing to notice, and they also can guide us in forming the questions that will broaden our behavioral zones of comfort.

Each of the four cells in the matrix in Figure 2 reflects a different set of behavioral preferences. The questions that follow automatically take you to each of the four cells. The regular asking and answering of questions such as these gradually expands your zone of comfort in behaving. That is, the questions expand your behavioral versatility. One aspect of effective leaders is that they automatically ask themselves questions such as these all the time.

1. *Deliberate Controlled:* What are the critical success factors for this operation? How shall we organize to maximize our success?

2. *Impulsive Controlled:* What do we need to be doing right now? What are the relevant time lines we must pay attention to?

3. *Deliberate Expressive:* Who are the best people for the job? How well have we built the team that will work on this project?

4. *Impulsive Expressive:* What are the potentials we could approach in this work? What is the larger context or rationale within which we are working?

As with the first model, each of us will most readily and automatically ask the questions from our most comfortable cells, and tend naturally to overlook those questions associated with our least comfortable cells.

Whenever we find ourselves resisting a change, or feel that we are spinning our wheels, questions such as these can lead to breakthroughs and progress. Each of us will have one or more favored quadrants which we "operate from" unconsciously most of the time. Any behavioral shifts out of the favored quadrant is unlikely unless we make a conscious choice to do so — or are faced with questions like those above, which force a shift in our awareness of the choices we are making.

QUESTIONS FOR CONTEMPLATION AND DIALOGUE

+ How can I live today to reflect my acceptance that tomorrow indeed does matter?

+ What can I do today to further positive change? Am I currently doing things to help build a sustainable tomorrow?

+ What am I doing to foster "inner" change in my outlook and reflections?

+ Can I more clearly connect my daily activities to a higher global purpose?

+ Do we believe that we can make any difference?

+ What are attractive and workable alternatives to self-indulgence and "eternal" growth?

+ What would be better terms than "growth" and "sustainability?"

+ Can we develop ways to explore these issues without making people feel guilty?

+ How do we learn to shift from "Us versus them" to "We're all in this together?"

+ How can our organizations learn to incorporate more long term, bigger picture thinking?

+ My/our activities are a means to what end?

TWO

Exponential Madness

~

"Human beings are like every other species in being able to reproduce beyond the carrying capacity of any finite habitat. Humans are like no other species in that they are capable of thinking about this fact and discovering its consequences."
WILLIAM R. CATTON, JR.

"Humanity is rapidly growing in size, in its use of resources, and in its production of waste; at rates that are not sustainable. The longer this continues, the lower the sustainable population and the lower the quality of life that will be possible."
DONELLA MEADOWS

I'm sure that nearly everyone who's reading this book has seen lots of exponential curves — they're in the newspapers and popular magazines virtually every issue. I'm equally certain that most people don't really understand the implications of these curves; nor do they have the awareness that *any* steady growth rate will follow an exponential path.

The Long Term/Big Picture Response

One way to get a sense of what is happening at a systems level around the world is to consider the curve below.[4] It describes the present rates of growth of a variety of processes, including: speed of travel, information published, number of technical journals, speed of computation, compound interest on savings, and agricultural production. More to the point of this book, the curve also describes: global population growth; amount of CO_2 released; percentage of population living in cities; percentage of GDP spent on arms by developing countries; desert area growth; loss of topsoil; generation of toxic waste; rate of rain forest destruction; rate of species loss; increase in debt financing; use of chemical fertilizers, pesticides and herbicides; and so on.

Figure 3 — Exponential Growth

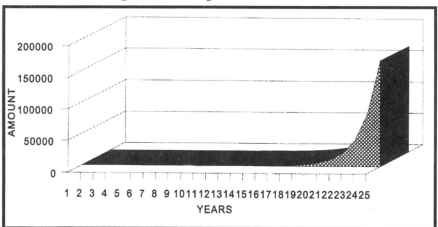

---

[4] The curve in Figure 3 was created by annually doubling the previous year's amount. The starting value in year 1 is 0.01. After 25 doublings, the value is 167,772.16

One has to wonder how much longer these rapid growth rates can continue, until they reach the various **"carrying capacities"** of the affected eco-systems. As these growth rates interact with each other, they have an expanded impact on the average person's everyday experience of work. An associate who recently resigned after 25 years as an executive in a large multinational corporation pointed out to me that, with the advent of lap top computers, the relevant cycle time for making business decisions had been compressed to 24 hours! That is, productivity and other goals were set each day, with pressure to "beat" the previous day. People who couldn't keep pace were told to clear out!

Understanding What "Doubling" Means

One of the best ways I know of to facilitate an understanding of exponential growth is to explore what happens when something doubles repeatedly. The often "automatic" idea is that when something is growing, say from 2 to 4, during a given period, say one year, that the growth the next year will be from 4 to 6. However, if the growth rate stays the same, the next year's growth will be to 8 rather than 6. Here is how an annual doubling would play out over years:

You'll get the point, I think, about how quickly things can get out of hand with an annual doubling. What was one "X" at the start becomes

```
YEAR

  0  x

  1  xx

  2  xxxx

  3  xxxxxxxx

  4  xxxxxxxxxxxxxxxx

  5  xxxxxxxxxxxxxxxxxxxxxxxxxxxxxxxx

  6  x x x x x x x x x x x x x x x x x x x x x x x x x x x x x x x x
     x x x x x x x x x x x x x x x x x x x x x x x x x x x x x x x x
```

256 "Xs" after only eight years! In another eight years, there would be 65,536 "Xs", and at the end of 25 years, 33,554,432 "Xs", far more "Xs" than there are characters in a good fat novel!

Another aspect of doublings that I think is important to understand is how long it takes for a quantity to double if you know the annual growth rate. There is a rather simple formula for this. If you know the annual percentage growth rate, divide this number into 70 for an approximate number of years to double the amount. For example, something that is growing at approximately 14% a year will double in size every five years.

The mental models and our related behavioral patterns that worked well when the above curve was relatively flat are obviously no longer serving us so well, now that the curve has become relatively steep.

Our worldwide economic system today is based on the imperative to "grow or die" and the imperative to do whatever we can do with our technological capabilities. When these imperatives cause problems, we readily assume that our technological prowess can be used to solve those problems.

What we are experiencing instead are diminishing returns from redoubled efforts to apply processes that aren't working well. Our choice to meet immediate needs for performance at the expense of longer term prospects for survival requires ever more effort! The result of this style of operating is that we are, increasingly, operating our enterprises as if the whole planet is a business in liquidation! It is likely that we are moving into a period which will be experienced as chaotic, as our old paradigm leads us to ever diminishing returns; and the emerging new paradigm is still taking shape.

We have an addiction to growth, deadlines and profits, to the extent that these processes have taken over our lives in ways we cannot control. Addictions cover up for emptiness and spiritual loss, and create a focus on a false communion with substitutes for being in the "here and now." This, in turn, leads to dulling routines and increasing incompatibilities with natural harmonies. And as with other addictions, a succession of crises begin to occur closer and closer together.

Most of us are oblivious to our addiction to growth, to "having" over "being." Our mass denial is based on our belief that we can continue on as we are, with no ill effects — the essence of this denial is an inner need to prevent awareness of any connection between our behavior and how it contributes to the inevitable consequences. As with all addictions, recovery requires a willingness to confront the pain that's being avoided — that all of this frenetic effort and deferred "being" is for naught.

It seems to me, and to most thoughtful futurists today, that to bring these growth rates under control, fundamental shifts in consciousness are necessary, and that if these shifts are not forthcoming in the very near future, the door of opportunity will slam shut irrevocably. Some of the shifts that are needed proceed from a narrow, short-term benefits outlook to one which includes a broad, long term purpose orientation. This shift needs to be accomplished while continuing to operate our enterprises — we can't really shut everything down while we reeducate and retool! A massive educational process is needed to develop a population-wide understanding of the big picture.

It is imperative that we also shift from our tendency to categorize, to make the "other" wrong, and to operate from an "either/or" mindset; to a much more relativistic/systemic, diversity appreciating, "both/and" mindset. And, to be sure, we must increase the emphasis on ethics in the operation of our organizations. The transition to a more benign way of living on the earth will create a period in which it is likely that many opportunists will see a chance to make their "fortunes" at the expense of everyone else. Thus we need to promulgate an ethical principle of "universalizability" — "Would it be right if everyone did it?" as a widely held test of whether or not to proceed on a proposed venture or engage in a suggested process.

There is also a fundamental shift that needs to take place in how we define growth. Today this term usually means "quantitative growth." A shift is needed to think of growth in qualitative terms. Initially this might mean that we measure growth in terms of quality of life rather than quantity of possessions. It would initially focus more energy on the replacement of infrastructure and environmentally unfriendly processes. Later, the priority will shift to growth in human qualities of dignity, integrity, and spirituality.

There are today two strategies for establishing a sustainable presence on the planet. Both are based on the notion that business is the only institution that is both globally situated and in a position to establish this sustainable presence. Governments, for example, are primarily focused on protecting their boundaries and enhancing the welfare of (at least some of) those who reside within those boundaries.

The first strategy suggests that businesses can tinker with what we are doing to solve the global problems we are daily being made aware of. This would involve recycling, reusing, inventing more efficient processes, cleaning up existing messes, conducting broad environmental audits, establishing "green" taxes, and the transfer of environment-enhancing technologies to developing nations.

The second strategy says that we must do all of these things, but that they are not in and of themselves sufficient to establish sustainability. This more radical strategy calls for a radical change in the global economic system which does away with debt based financing and reflects the environmental costs of extraction and processing. It calls for GDP to be based on many social dimensions in addition to economic activities; and for huge increases in humanistic, spiritual, and ecological values. Further, "What benefits?" must be replaced by "What purpose?" and "economic development" by "human development."

I also believe that this second strategy needs to be based on continuous learning. If we are to handle the pressures attendant on exponential growth then surely we need to be learning at an exponential rate also. Yesterday's solutions will probably prove insufficient to the challenges of tomorrow's complex, intertwined pressures.

Some Implications

There are many practical things that can be undertaken in our organizations now that will help us address the long term situation described in the previous paragraphs. Here are some suggestions you can immediately implement without great cost.

We can undertake dialogues in our organizations to determine what **strategy** to adopt. These strategies could range from fixing existing environmental and/or community based conditions; to compliance with regulations; to active prevention; to a full community wide program of ecological sustainability. Assessments of savings to be realized through increased efficiency can make any given strategy more cost effective. Groups can also begin looking into the competitive advantages of undertaking audits to identify healthier ways of functioning in the marketplace. Further, sustainability task forces (or **Stakeholder Councils**) could look into the implications of the previously described impending problems for many areas of the corporation: 1) leadership, 2) strategy formulation, 3) organization, 4) human resources policies, 5) information processing, 6) control systems, 7) public affairs stances, 8) manufacturing processes, 9) marketing approaches, 10) technology utilization, and 11) financial practices.

Further, each organization could establish **principles** for its operations, relative to long term ecological security, human resources security, and socio-economic security. Once you have established these principles, you can undertake explorations to establish internal transformations in business practices, structures and operating functions; and external transformations relative to relationships with political, regulatory, economic/fiscal, and social entities.

Questions For Contemplation And Dialogue

- ✧ How do I maintain my awareness of the growing global challenges and not get so overwhelmed that I turn off and go back to business as usual?

- ✧ Who's to say that this is not just another alarmist reaction?

- ✧ What role can I play in supporting business leaders (and share holders) to care about more than growth?

✧ What do I consider to be the most critical challenges, and what can I contribute to their resolution?

✧ How do we overcome the widespread greediness and belief in scarcity?

✧ How much stuff is enough?

✧ What are our answers to the Iroquois Nation's challenge to consider the impact of our daily work activities on the seventh generation to come?

✧ If I did everything "right," would that be enough?

✧ If the corporations in my community grow at an average annual rate of 3% (or 5%, 10%, 15%), what will be the impacts on resources, waste, community life, and the local environment?

✧ What are the implications of chaos theory for the establishment of a sustainable consciousness?

✧ How can we create sufficient dissatisfaction with the way things are in order to motivate change?

THREE

The Financial System
Has The Tallest Buildings

"Business has become, in the last half of the 20th century, the most powerful institution on the planet. The dominant institution in any society needs to take responsibility for the whole. This is a new role for business, not yet well understood or accepted."

WILLIS HARMAN

"The next challenge for all international business leaders is to develop a new world vision — a form of business ethic which sees this commitment to good corporate citizenship as a natural part of business practice."

H.R.H. PRINCE CHARLES, THE PRINCE OF WALES

As Willis Harman pointed out on many occasions, throughout Western history the dominant institution in society has taken responsibility for its entire sphere of influence. Until about 400 years ago, before the days of Galileo, Copernicus, and Newton, the Church was the dominant institution in society, and it took responsibility for all aspects of human experience within its sphere of influence. In its heyday, the Holy Roman Empire ruled most of what we now know as Europe, and the Pope was more or less responsible for everything within the realm.

Joseph Campbell told us that the dominant institution in a society tends to build the tallest buildings, and the Church's cathedral spires towered over the landscape in those days. After the "Copernican Revolution" however, the national governments rapidly became the dominant institutions in the West, and Government buildings defined the peaks in the urban skyline. Government leaders, first genealogically determined and then elected, took responsibility for all aspects of the human experience.

Today it's obvious when approaching any city who has the tallest buildings. The financial system now defines the urban skyline worldwide, and the practice of business has become the dominant activity everywhere. To date, however, business takes responsibility first for its own short term profitability (share holder interest!), and only a little energy overall is invested into the larger concerns of the community. The current practice of business, with its focus on short cycle profitability, calls into question whether or not it is even possible for business to assume this wider responsibility.

Business still expects government to be responsible for all human activities and experiences that don't flow to their bottom lines. Business also expects government to keep up the infrastructure and make sure that all supportive non-business systems are functioning well. Governments maintain military forces in large part to protect the economic activities of business. But when the government tries to protect the environment, sometimes causing businesses increased costs, many business leaders look for loopholes or attempt to have the laws changed in ways that will be more favorable to corporate net profits.

To be fair, most larger businesses around the world recognize the need for environmental restraint and so maintain compliance with regulations intended to protect the environment. This, however, does not go far enough, as the regulations themselves are rooted in some unsustainable and, as yet, largely untested assumptions – that we can somehow find a way to go on growing indefinitely and that doing a little better than we have in the past will be sufficient. Most businesses won't (can't?) go beyond compliance unless there is a "business case" for doing so ... i.e. the added steps lead to increased profitability.

The next evolutionary step in human consciousness will lead to businesses that naturally move beyond compliance to anticipation and prevention of ecological or social degradations; and then on to ecological and social "capacity building" as their natural modes of operating. The challenge we all face ultimately is whether or not this evolutionary development of perspective (or consciousness) will occur rapidly enough to create the kind of future each of us would describe as the ideal one for our own grandchildren.

There has been little doubt during the 20th century that the role of private enterprise is to meet the needs of society and to generate wealth. With the rapid growth of speculative investing during the last quarter of this century, shareholder equity has become the call to action and increasing numbers of senior executives have received hundreds of thousands of shares of their companies' stock in order to "help" them stay focused on the financial performance of the company, and to diminish other concerns from their focuses.

There are increasing signs that fundamental transformations are underway. Among the presumed positive trends are the emergence of a single, global economy and marketplace, enormous technological advancement, and instantaneous global communications.

Additional signs that change is coming appear to be less positive: ongoing degradation of the natural environment; a rapidly widening gap between rich and poor as wealth is being concentrated among fewer and fewer people;[5] and increasing worldwide unemployment, underemployment, and homelessness.

---

[5] The net worth of the world's wealthiest 500 individuals today exceeds the net worth of the world's poorest 3,000,000,000 individuals (a 6,000,000 to 1 ratio).

The future state of the world, whatever it is, will most certainly depend on how these various trends unfold, along with the likely emergence of new trends and unexpected surprises. Whatever the future, it seems quite safe to assume that business practices will have a strong influence on the world of the 21st century. Decline into chaos is in no way assured; nor is a smooth slide into some utopian state. What *is* needed is a soul searching enquiry into what is driving both the opportunities and the challenges.

The premise throughout this book is that the eventual results produced by the trends cited will ultimately be the results supported by the perspectives, or mind sets, of a critical mass of the global population. An individual's perspective is made up of his or her beliefs, expectations, and assumptions. Most of us have spent very little time becoming aware of the perspectives we hold and how we learned them. This lack of awareness of our perspectives and their roots does not in any way diminish their generative role in strongly influencing the qualities that emerge in the future. *Our choice to be conscious or unconscious about our individual and collective impact on whatever future our children and grandchildren are to inherit from us.*

Some of the largely untested assumptions driving today's global realities are:

- ✧ Continuous economic growth is essential for human progress.
- ✧ Continuous technological advancement is essential for human progress.
- ✧ Business should not be expected to pay for the depletion of the natural resources it consumes, nor for the disposal of the attendant wastes.
- ✧ There is no compelling reason to question the continuing concentration of wealth and patterns of ownership.
- ✧ Technology can be counted on to take care of ecological challenges when they eventually get bad enough to pay attention to.

◇ Free markets result in the most efficient and progressive ways to operate.

◇ Economic globalization is generally good for almost everyone.

(HARMAN AND PORTER, 1997)

A growing number of business leaders and business thinkers are concluding that these assumptions, and others like them, are at the heart of the challenges described throughout this book. They are also arguing that these challenges are merely early symptoms of a more fundamental disorder — a disorder of perspective — the perspective held today by a critical mass of humanity.

A listing of a few recent business book titles indicates the emerging concerns about our present style of conducting business.

◇ *The New Business of Business: Sharing Responsibility for a Positive Global Future.* Willis Harman and Maya Porter (eds.), 1997.

◇ *Leadership in a New Era: Visionary Approaches to the Biggest Crisis of Our Time.* John Renesch (ed.), 1994.

◇ *The End of Work: The Global Labor Force and the Dawn of the Post Market Era.* Jeremy Rifkin, 1995.

◇ *Stewardship: Choosing Service over Self Interest.* Peter Block, 1996.

◇ *Changing Course: Report of the Business Council for Sustainable Development.* Stephan Schmidheiny, 1992.

◇ *The Growth Illusion: How Economic Growth has Enriched the Few, Impoverished the Many, and Endangered the Planet.* R. Douthwaite, 1992.

◇ *When Corporations Rule the World.* David Korten, 1995.

◇ *Leading with Soul.* Lee Bolman & Terry Deal, 1995.

◇ *The New Paradigm in Business.* Michael Ray & Alan Rinzler (eds.), 1993.

- ✧ *The New Bottom Line: Bringing Heart and Soul to Business.* John Renesch & B. DeFoore (eds.), 1996.

- ✧ *Heart at Work.* Jack Canfield & Jacqueline Miller, 1996.

- ✧ *Reawakening Spirit at Work.* Jack Hawley, 1993.

Also, some of the indications that all is not well are chronicled by Harman and Porter (1997). These include:

- ✧ The on-going systematic destruction of the natural environment

- ✧ Loss of a sense of community world-wide.

- ✧ Systematic "upward" transfer of wealth.

- ✧ Wide spread marginalization of individuals and cultures.

- ✧ On-going erosion and denial of the spiritual aspects of life.

- ✧ Learned sense of incapacity and helpfulness.

While humane, spiritual, and nature loving values are becoming increasingly commonplace at the individual level, (P. Ray, 1996), they clearly are still subordinated to economic growth values at the levels of the corporation and the economy. In Chapter 10, I suggest that as these values continue to grow in the population, a new, more custodial mind set will attain critical mass.

Clearly, any major shift in present directions will require the involvement of our dominant institutions. Students of systems dynamics are well aware of the "delivery delay" aspect of system functioning. What this means is that the eventual outcomes of complex social or ecological systems operations occur at some time *after* those outcomes have become nonreversible. That is, there is some point prior to a given system result after which the result is inevitable.

Systems thinking teaches us that the social and ecological "outcomes" (as of, say, 2030), of the present trends will be "fixed" at some point prior to 2030. There are too many complex variables involved to specify exactly the date of the "point of no return," but there is no doubt that it will occur a few years to several years earlier than 2030. What is most critical in this is the degree to which the dominant institutions correctly interpret and proactively respond *prior* to that unspecifiable point of no return.

Obviously, business will play a crucial role in all of this, whether it does so consciously or unconsciously. Much will depend on people with emerging, broad, ecological, and spiritual perspectives assuming decision-making positions in mainstream institutions. As will be described in Chapter 10, such a subculture is growing rapidly, but at present tends to shun mainstream institutional life and is, for the most part, unaware of the immensity of its growing, but still latent power to influence life on earth. As this subculture continues to spread, new ways of thinking will naturally emerge that will embrace the needed larger sense of responsibility for the whole.

At the present time, a large portion of those who are early adopters of these new ways of thinking are working in small businesses or are self employed. If they do belong to larger institutions, they most often belong to voluntary and nonprofit associations called NonGovernmental Organizations, or NGOs. Often these NGOs are today working *against* mainstream businesses and are therefore seen by business leaders as nettlesome and irrelevant to the true concerns of business.

However, I know from first hand experience that there are large numbers of people working diligently in large, mainstream corporations today who are also thinking in these new ways. They get little reward, and sometimes much ridicule, for their perspectives. Often, they don't know how many allies they have in their companies and/or are unwilling to risk their careers by speaking out.

As these "new thinkers" (referred to as Cultural Creatives by Paul Ray (1996) and described in the final chapter of this book) learn to recognize each other, and as they move into decision making and policy formulating positions, new corporate visions are likely. Companies like Tom's of Maine and Ben & Jerry's are perhaps the early harbingers of what may emerge over the next few decades to become the predominant style of business. Alliances between businesses and NGOs will rapidly become commonplace as community building and longer term sustainability rise to the top of corporate priority lists.

Questions For Contemplation And Dialogue

✧ If our organizations all got everything they wanted, what would our world look like?

✧ How can we reconcile short term needs of having jobs that help businesses grow, when this does not appear to be sustainable in the long run?

✧ If we humans created a system in which growth is essential, couldn't we also create a new system in which long term quality of life is essential?

✧ If business won't take responsibility for the whole, who will emerge to hold everyone in mind?

✧ What might replace quantitative growth as the pre-eminent goal of business?

✧ How can I help my organization take a more global, longer term view?

✧ How can we influence our organizations to consider the questions of future impact?

✧ How can we bring more attention to the emerging external challenges into the everyday operations of our organizations?

✧ How can we better reward integrity and ethical practice at work?

✧ How can we foster continuous dialogue and deep conversations about sustainable consciousness?

✧ To what extent am I willing and able to educate/confront my organization about inhumane and unethical practices?

✧ How can we help our organizations factor in larger, more pervasive issues?

✧ What support systems are needed for organizations of all kinds to find meaning beyond the bottom line?

✧ How can we help our organizations identify true value from a systemic long-term perspective?

✧ How can we raise human values to become a measure of business success?

⋄ How do we get the attention of the CEOs and other key decision makers?

⋄ How can we help business leaders connect directly with people outside of their direct business sphere — especially children and the elderly?

⋄ How do I reconcile working for an organization that operates in inherently unsustainable ways but has a broad humanitarian purpose driving it?

⋄ Is sustainable consciousness even possible in an organization in crisis? Is survival possible without sustainable consciousness?

⋄ Can we bring children to board meetings, shareholder meetings, planning meetings?

⋄ Can we help our organizations make children's upbringing a line item?

⋄ How should we be advising the organizations we work with about the ways they're doing business that may be having a negative impact on our world 30 years from now?

⋄ How can we link organizational incentives to activities that promote sustainable consciousness?

⋄ Can we benchmark people and programs that are working successfully with sustainable consciousness?

⋄ Who will lead the process of encouraging leaders at all levels to create visions, policies, and mechanisms that reflect and call forth a sustainable consciousness?

⋄ Can we create a community wide industry forum to address sustainable consciousness?

⋄ How should I respond to lack of awareness/detrimental behaviors in others?

⋄ How do we distinguish between "good" people and "bad" systems?

Section II

We Can't Resolve
Any of These Challenges
We Can Only Resolve All of Them!

In HIS BOOK, *IN OUR FACE*, PSYCHOLOGIST JOHN ENRIGHT (1993) PROPOSES that:

> *"We can't solve any of these problems, we can only solve all of them. We can't save ourselves, we can only save everyone."*

Our present way of looking for relatively easy solutions to relatively simple challenges cannot get to the root of what is unfolding at the level of complex systems. The best we can hope for is superficially treating symptoms. Even addressing today's challenges at the level of entire disciplines, such as ecology or economics, can only address symptoms.

In order to secure a sustainable future, I believe that we must address these challenges with very broad systems thinking which incorporates ecology *and* economics *and* population growth *and* human consciousness. Only when we begin to see, on a regular day to day basis, how these factors interact with each other (*and* with other factors as well) will we be able to tackle the fundamental changes needed to ensure a sustainable, high quality human existence.

Historically, humanity has shown itself to be highly resilient and adaptive at major crisis points. When in the midst of major changes, I am sure that the picture looks pretty bleak to those who are experiencing it. Take, for example, the transformation to a global, information driven marketplace. Those in the United States whose careers have been situated in declining industries have had to endure huge amounts of suffering and have often seen their life long dreams shattered. But when we look back from the future, this industrial transformation will probably be recorded in history books as having been easily accomplished, just a mere ripple in the human psyche.

The prevailing economic "laws" and models place little or no *future* value on a forest, a cache of mineral ore, or a family of whales. These and other "resources" (from the point of view that humans own the earth and should do whatever they like with it) have value only when consumed as a part of an economic transaction today. The basic understanding that we have adopted in our economic lives is "to go on consuming until there is nothing left to consume."

Likewise, the prevailing "laws" of many world religions frown on curtailing birth rates and, in many parts of the world, large families are the surest form of "social security" available. If today's global birth rate were sustainable, the weight of the human population would exceed the weight of the earth in a few hundred years. Of course, since our physical bodies are made from the earth and have to be sustained by foods also made from the earth, this clearly will be impossible, unless we send huge numbers into space!

The three chapters in this section explore what it might take, in the areas of ecology, economics, and population, in order to establish an acceptable quality of life for future generations. Section three then addresses the fourth factor — human consciousness.

Questions For Contemplation And Dialogue

✧ Is it already too late? Why should I bother?

✧ What magnitude of changes should I/can I/will I make?

✧ How do we discover our interconnectedness across organizations, communities, nations, and disciplines?

✧ What questions can we pose that will be shocking enough to stimulate the needed changes?

✧ How must we operate to build long term sustainable capability instead of only patching up current systems?

✧ How can we redefine growth in ways that are economically, ecologically, and demographically sound?

✧ How can we have a collective impact on the major challenges that require more than narrow, parochial responses?

✧ How can greater attention to diversity help us to foster sustainable consciousness?

✧ What can I teach the children?

✧ How am I contributing to the future in the way that I am raising my children?

FOUR

Mother Nature Will Be Just Fine

"Modern humanity is rapidly destroying the natural world on which it depends for survival. If current trends persist, in a few decades the biosphere will cease to be capable of supporting complex forms of life."

EDWARD GOLDSMITH

"Look around you — everything you see is "stolen goods." You haven't paid the full price for anything you own because the resources that were extracted and the pollution that was created to produce those goods were considered to be free. But they aren't free. Have you recently received a bill for the oxygen you use? You should, because there is a real cost; especially if you turn it into carbon dioxide. How many thousands of trees would you have to plant to regenerate the oxygen you use and reabsorb the carbon dioxide you are responsible for using?"

ECKART WINTZEN

"We find ourselves, one way or another, in the midst of a large scale experiment to change the chemical construction of the stratosphere, even though we have no clear idea of what the biological or meteorological consequences may be."

F. SHERWOOD ROWLAND

In *The Ecology of Commerce*, Paul Hawken (1993) points out that the biosphere that supports all life on the planet is roughly equivalent to a thin layer of paint sprayed on a basketball! At present, most if not all of the challenges to this thin and fragile biosphere are created by human activity, reflect human beliefs and values, and have arisen from perfectly legal operations. Many believe that we are rapidly making the planet uninhabitable without breaking any laws. The laws of nature, which include the second law of thermodynamics (all material disperses — or — "stuff" spreads) and the law of conservation of matter and energy (no matter is ever lost — or — "stuff" doesn't go away) are going to operate regardless of which ways the political winds blow.

For centuries before it was possible, mankind wanted to fly. There were probably thousands of failures, costing thousands of lives, prior to the 19th century successes with hot air balloons and early 20th century successes with heavier-than-air flying machines. The laws of aerodynamics are now relatively well understood — we think. But they did not spring into existence in order to be discovered in the last hundred or so years — they were operating all along, regardless of our level of understanding of them!

It is safe to assume, I think, that there are still undiscovered ecological "laws" which are operating in the absence of human understanding. And even the ones we do understand, we often violate for the sake of short term human self interest (i.e. profits this quarter). So once again my question regarding the biosphere is this: "Will it ever be appropriate for human activity to take a more preventive stance towards the health of the environment?" If the answer is "yes," then my second question becomes: "When is the last moment that we can do this and still maintain a reasonable quality of existence?"

Chief Oren Lyons, of the Onondaga Nation, is among those who differentiate the "world," which is a man made economic-political entity, from the "planet," which, except for inputs from the sun, is a closed physical system with a fragile ability to support life. He often points out that the planet will survive very nicely, and that the natural laws will continue to operate in spite of what we may do. Even if we were to destroy life as we know it on the planet with our activities, life might eventually return — there would be grass, and trees, and eventually, animals again. It is the "world" that human activity threatens, not the "planet."

As we will see below, Chief Lyons may not be right after all. After a certain amount of time, a point of no return would be reached, beyond which life forms as we know them could not continue to exist. If we assume that today's species are all at the pinnacle of their evolution, it then follows that, after starting over, the grasses, trees, and animals might evolve very differently! And it may take an incomprehensible amount of time for this to happen.

Working from this perspective since the mid-1980's, Swedish doctor Karl-Henrik Robèrt has articulated a fundamental set of four nonnegotiable system conditions which must be met if we are to maintain a human presence on the Earth. He refers to them as *The Natural Step*. Dr. Robèrt, a distinguished cancer researcher, physician, and creator of The Natural Step Foundation, has had a lifelong interest in the quality of life that future generations can expect.

He became frustrated when he reviewed the work of environmentalists and found that most progress was blocked by disagreements over details and short term agenda differences. It seemed obvious to him that there must be some fundamental truths based on scientific knowledge that would be accepted by everyone, no matter what their political, social, or economic beliefs. Using a vivid metaphor, Dr. Robèrt suggests that most of these discussions are like monkeys chattering in the leaves of the tree of life, rather than addressing the challenges being experienced by the roots and trunk of the tree.

As a result, he wrote a paper that attempted to foresee and circumvent the problems people most often have in reaching a consensus. After a process of consensus building that involved twenty-one manuscript revisions, Dr. Robèrt was able to achieve consensus among fifty prominent Swedish scientists on an initial educational package that presented fundamental truths to which we must adhere if we are to maintain a high quality human presence on the planet. From this consensus paper, Dr. Robèrt, with the help of the King of Sweden and numerous business leaders, created an illustrated booklet and an audio cassette that was mailed to every household and every educational institution in Sweden.

Dr. Robèrt was able to persuade a number of major companies, cities, and trade unions of the outstanding properties of this project, and Sweden's King agreed to become a patron of the project. With outstanding early success, The Natural Step Foundation was officially launched in the spring of 1989. The foundation is made up of a network of experts from many fields. They serve as bridge builders working to establish consensus understandings of the non-negotiable truths in a large number of fields and industries, such as agriculture and energy. One outstanding feature of The Natural Step process is that, unlike many other similar groups, it is nonadversarial in its approach, preferring to find areas of agreement and to build consensus rather than forcing change.

The ultimate purpose of The Natural Step Foundation is to uncover common ground where all people can meet. When all can agree on a set of scientific facts, and on the logical implications for those facts, the path is more likely to be cleared for concrete action. Agreements are developed, and good examples are rewarded, using appreciative processes that continuously seek new insights and ask for advice from all critics. Most of the energy expended by The Natural Step Foundation in support of those businesses that are eager to bring their processes into accord with the four basic system conditions, confident in the idea that when 15-20% of the population gets behind a new idea, its general adoption becomes inevitable. This is the same as my ideas about "preaching to the choir," which is described later on, in Section III. Our hope for the future, I firmly believe, is the global emergence of a critical mass of networked "new thinkers."

The Natural Step

Dr. Robèrt often begins his presentations by showing a photograph of the Earth, taken by Apollo astronauts while on the moon, and asking his audience how many people think that the Earth is gaining weight. When none of the people raise their hands, he then asks them how many think that the Earth is losing weight. Again, no hands go up. He then congratulates his audience for understanding the law of conservation of matter and energy, which suggests that the total number of atoms on the planet, give or take a meteorite or two, is fixed — unchanging. We clearly already know this at some level.

He then goes on to ask people what would happen if a large box — closed and perfectly insulated — could be placed around their metropolitan area, enclosing the region completely for a number of years. Everyone easily agrees that when the box is eventually opened, there will be no life, lots of waste product, and an even temperature throughout. Within a relatively short period, all of the resources are consumed in meeting human survival needs. In other words, entropy (and junk) always increase in a closed system, and after a certain point, life cannot be sustained. In getting this point, the audience demonstrates that it already understands the second law of thermodynamics, which suggests that materials and energy disperse continuously.

Another way to visualize these laws is to imagine a bathtub filled with water. If you put a drop of dark blue ink in the water, it would disperse and seem to disappear completely. Yet all of its atoms are still present. If you put enough drops of ink into the water, the water eventually will turn blue, and you could neither use the ink for writing, nor the water for drinking. With no loss of matter, the quality of each substance is diminished beyond usability.

"So then what?" asks Dr. Robèrt. "In light of these two laws of physics, accepted without question for over 100 years, what does it mean that our garbage dumps are growing and our population is growing and our resources are being used up and dispersed into visible and molecular junk at an increasing rate?" All of this happens without the Earth gaining or losing any atoms — which means that our usable resources are being depleted and that waste is steadily accumulating. Therefore, the resource potential for health and economy is systematically decreasing.

This can be portrayed as a funnel that is narrowing with the passage of time — as a result of resource depletion, accumulation of junk in the environment, and relentless population growth. The real question we must all address, whether we are householders or corporate executives or government employees, is "How do we keep moving ahead, as the funnel narrows, rather than crashing against the sides of the funnel?"

Figure 4 — Funnel of Opportunity

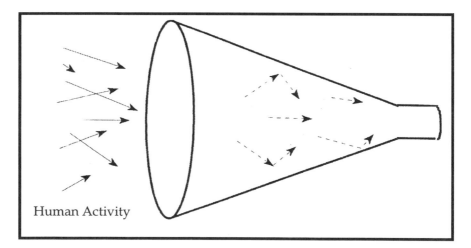

Human Activity

While matter and energy are neither created nor destroyed on Earth, the *quality and utility* of matter and energy can be created or destroyed. "Mother Nature's" cycles have served as a quality building machine for approximately three and a half billion years. We have decided to call the ongoing creation of quality "evolution." Throughout the history of the planet, there has been a movement away from "dispersed junk" and towards increasing "quality." Plant cells eventually were created and "learned" how to build quality through photosynthesis.

All processes other than those fueled by the sun, of which photosynthesis is the dominant one, consume this quality and create junk. If it weren't for the sun and the photosynthesis it stimulates, which helps the Earth to not be a completely closed system, our planet would soon end up like the city in a box described a few paragraphs back. The factor is the Sun, which adds its energy to "Mother Nature's Quality Machine" through the process of photosynthesis. As a result, throughout the eons, the net production of photosynthesis has exceeded the consumption of quality, and evolution has proceeded, not always smoothly, through various stages including, most recently, the appearance of humans and the onset of human activity on the planet.

Figure 5 — The Quality Building Nature of Photosynthesis

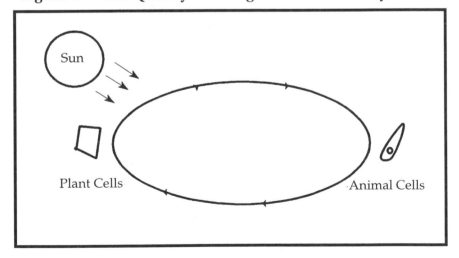

Herein lies a huge challenge. As the latest step in the process of evolution, we humans have tried to delude ourselves into thinking that evolutionary processes have ended with us — that everything "lower" on the scale "belongs" to us, that evolution has ended and we are a "finished product." In fact, there are relatively few factors that differentiate human cells from the most primitive plant cells. In order to tell the difference between a human cell and virtually any other animal cell, you have to get down to the level of molecules! Most likely, we are not the end of an evolutionary chain, we are just another facet of nature itself!

We can portray any "modern" human activity (4 in Figure 6), from running a household to operating a factory, as a cycle within the quality building cycle of nature. In order to operate, we usually consume quality from the quality building machine, reducing the net product of photosynthesis by, for example, cutting forests or paving over green areas (3 in Figure 6), and we consume resources from the crust of the earth, for example, through extraction of petroleum and ores (1 in Figure 6).

Figure 6 — Human Activity in the EcoSystem

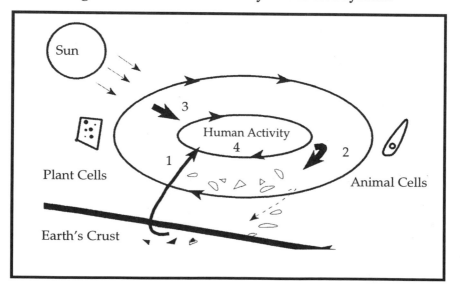

These activities create dispersed visible and molecular junk (2 in Figure 6). (If you doubt this, ask yourself where the fumes from your car go — nothing disappears — or what would happen to your car over time if you didn't wax it? As the treads on your car's tires wear away, the rubber doesn't disappear from the face of the earth). Since very little of this junk can be easily or quickly reabsorbed into the earth's crust as usable material, it gradually accumulates, sooner or later becoming toxic to life forms.

As a result, overall quality is diminished, and the pattern of evolution reverses to become "devolution," back towards the uninhabitable state of the earth in its earliest stages of development. Over the past few centuries, human activity has far exceeded the cleansing and restorative capacities of the quality machine — actually reversing evolution!

How can anyone feel that it is legitimate to say "So far, so good" just because we have not yet experienced severe consequences from the activities we have already been engaged in? The eternal violation of any of the essential principles of sustainability will eventually lead to what humans call a disaster. However, what we may never be able to tell is when, where, and how much, because there are too many complex factors to be considered. If these considerations represent the leaves in the tree; the unsustainability of violating any of the system conditions represents the trunk of the tree. Anything will become toxic if it is concentrated enough. Mother Nature cannot absorb forever increasing dispersed junk.

The Four Non-Negotiable System Conditions

Dr. Robèrt crystallized the following system conditions in his consensus building process. They arise from the two laws of physics mentioned earlier that all matter disperses, and that no matter is ever lost. Any violation of these four system conditions leads to the accumulation of visible and molecular junk, and contributes to the process of reverse evolution (devolution).

System condition number one: *We must not base our economies on extracting mineral and petroleum deposits from the crust of the earth at a faster rate than the natural cycles are able to reconcentrate them* (1 in Figure 6). Since atoms are never lost, everything that is withdrawn from the Earth's reserves has to end up somewhere. Therefore, extracted minerals will accumulate as waste, either solid or molecular, for as long as the extraction rate is greater than the Earth's ability to reconcentrate them as ores or petroleum.

This, of course, means extremely severe restrictions on oil and mineral extraction — which is not a popular idea among mining and petroleum companies. Nevertheless, there are by definition finite limits on these materials and we can expect the population to double over the next few decades, leading to radically increased demands. The faster we consume and create trash, the "healthier" we consider ourselves to be economically. It is likely that we will experience the toxic side effects of this process, e.g. cadmium in our kidneys, or overwhelming costs arising from the destruction of natural resources.

System condition number two: *We must cease the release of persistent unnatural (i.e. synthetic) compounds into the environment* (2 in Figure 6). A high percentage of manufacturing processes today involve the production or utilization of man-made materials that are chemically complex and do not occur naturally in nature. Following the two undisputed laws of physics (things disperse and things don't go away), these materials are like drops of ink in a bathtub full of water. For a long time, we aren't aware of them, but eventually, the water turns blue (e.g. we discover toxic chemicals in the milk of the mother polar bear).

The phenomenon of the annually increasing ozone layer holes is a perfect example of system condition number two. When Chloro-Fluoro-Carbons (CFCs) were invented, they were celebrated as a wondrous achievement of modern chemistry. CFCs made modern refrigeration economically possible for the masses. They also allowed us to learn to take air conditioning for granted in a very short period of time.

It was thought that their stability meant that they would not pollute the environment. In short, CFCs were considered to be an incredible example of the now out of favor advertising slogan "better living through chemistry."

It is the very stability and persistence of synthetic substances that are the eventual cause of difficulty. The stable CFCs rise slowly up to the ozone layer, over a period of 25 to 50 years. Once there, the chlorine atoms are released and each one breaks down ozone molecules for a very long period of time — estimated at from 50 to 150 years for each CFC molecule!. Only a small portion of the CFCs that have been released into the atmosphere have arrived at the ozone layer to date, and we are already experiencing severe consequences — especially in the Southern Hemisphere. Even in North America and Europe, however, dermatologists are reporting an extremely rapid increase in skin cancer rates, presumably related to the thinning ozone layer worldwide. There is no way to know for sure what consequences we may already have unleashed on the next generation from this one family of synthetics alone. Once again, it is not justifiable to say "so far, so good."

Many of the thousands of synthetics in use around the globe today are not biodegradable; that is, breaking them down into their original components is either impossible or takes a very long time. While scientists and politicians continue to squabble over safe thresholds for this dispersed junk, it continues to accumulate far more rapidly than most of us realize.

There are too many complexities operating for us to be able to establish when, where, and how much toxicity to expect, but we do know that the amounts are growing every minute. Metaphorically, it is like getting down on our hands and knees to mop up the floor because the sink has begun to overflow. As long as we have spare towels for the mopping, we might not think to stand up and turn off the tap!

System condition three: *We must not reduce the natural biological cycle in its production of "life" through the process of photosynthesis* (3 in Figure 6). Ecologists refer to the excess production of green cells, beyond what the plants need for themselves, as the Net Product of Photosynthesis (NPP). They estimate that human activity today is consuming just over 40% of the NPP in any given year, and that our rate of consumption, especially through paving over green space and burning rain forests, is growing rapidly.

As noted earlier, in the chapter "Exponential Madness," we can find the approximate doubling time in years of a growth rate by dividing the annual growth rate percentage into the number 70. So, for example, if we increase our utilization and/or destruction of NPP at a rate of 5% annually, we will be doubling the amount of NPP consumed annually by human activity to 80% of the total in only 14 years. Clearly, as the population continues to grow, we will experience the consequences of too little remaining NPP within a very short period of time! And this does not even take into account that the physical environment becomes more impoverished in any area that is heavily populated by humans.

Here again, as scientists and politicians quibble about where, when and how much impact there will be, the NPP is being inexorably reduced by human activity. The symptoms we are already experiencing include growing deserts, loss of topsoil, rapid species loss, and increasing salinity of farmlands.

System condition number four: *The "metabolism" of human activities* (4 in Figure 6) *must not exceed the capacity of nature to maintain balance with respect to the first three conditions, our economies must be efficient and fair with regard to the amount of resources needed to meet human needs.* We must improve our efficiencies with respect to the use of extracted minerals and fuels from the Earth's crust (system condition number one). We must become more natural and efficient in our manufacturing processes, in order to not produce synthetics and other wastes faster than the Earth can process them (system condition number two). And we must be less destructive of and more efficient in our utilization of renewable (i.e. green) natural resources (system condition number three). Most of the other chapters in this book delve into what it will take to actually satisfy system condition four.

At the present time we are, in the words of economist Herman Daly (1991), operating our economies as if the Earth were a business in liquidation. However, the system we have invented to measure our "success" is so deeply entrenched in our psyches that very few of us are willing or able to seriously call it into question. To do so would be to realize that what we have considered to be our fundamental reality, especially since the Second World War, is really a very shortsighted illusion. And even though this illusion cannot persist much longer, we cling tightly to it, hoping that the technology will somehow be invented which will circumvent the end of life as we know it.

What Shall We Do?

There is no argument that the four system conditions are essential to maintaining life as we know it. While we may easily debate the details of how long we can delay before acting, it should be patently obvious that some very fundamental changes are required. The sooner we begin acting, the easier it will be to avoid forced solutions. In the terms of the "funnel" portrayed in Figure 4, the sides of the funnel will stop narrowing for a given enterprise at the point at which that enterprise satisfies the four system conditions.

When people first encounter the four basic system conditions for sustainability, they quite naturally seek ways to deny or circumvent the conditions rather than gladly giving up a life style they take as a right rather than as a luxury borrowed from the future. It is also quite natural that people immediately see obstacles to achieving the conditions. Consider, for example, the amount of capital investment (and people's pension funds) tied up in petrochemicals. People frequently ask "How could we just walk away from that?"

Dr. Robèrt suggests that we not even think about leaping all the way to the goals of compliance with the essential conditions. He also cautions against doing nothing because the tasks initially seem overwhelming. There are always, according to Dr. Robèrt, at least a few things that can be done immediately to move in the direction of the goals. If "we" start taking obvious steps in the direction of the goals now, while there is still at least a little discretionary time, we are likely to invent ways to overcome the obstacles as we approach them.

Figure 7 — Moving in the Direction of Our Goals

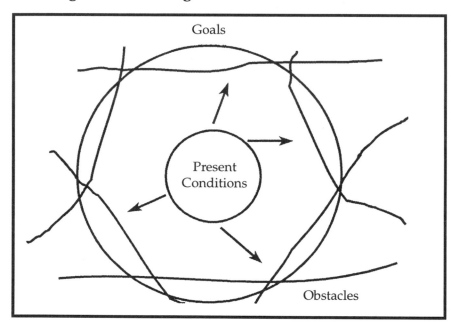

Since our economic activity is driven by business enterprises, the business community has a major responsibility in moving us all towards compliance with the essential system conditions. Those businesses that have taken up the challenge are finding that even though the short term development costs of more sustainable products might be high, longer term profitability is greater.

There is some very good news in this regard. A number of businesses and cities in Sweden have already undertaken The Natural Step process and are experiencing great success in moving towards the goals they have set for themselves in relation to the four system conditions for sustainability. Most notable among these are IKEA, a furniture manufacturer, and Electrolux, a home appliance manufacturer. It has also been adopted by the Swedish Farmer's Federation and by over 40 Swedish cities. To date, over two dozen professional networks have been formed in Sweden to support The Natural Step, including: Scientists for the Environment, Engineers for the Environment, Artists for the Environment, and Management Consultants for the Environment. (Several thousand people are involved in these networks). The Natural Step is also picking up momentum in several European countries, and more recently, in the United States.

I want to close this chapter with *The Earth Prayer* from the United Nations Environmental Sabbath Program.

> We join with the earth and with each other
> to bring new life in the land,
> to restore the water,
> to refresh the air.
> We join with the earth and with each other
> to renew the forests,
> to care for the plants,
> to protect the creatures.
>
> We join with the earth and with each other
> to recreate the human community,
> to promote justice and peace,
> to remember our children.
> We join with the earth and with each other.
> We join together as many and diverse expressions of one loving mystery;
> for the healing of the earth and the renewal of all life.

Questions For Contemplation And Dialogue

✧ What do we mean by "Nature's Plan," and do we think that we are separate from it?

✧ What is the present environmental perspective of most people in my field or line of work?"

✧ How could we bring the values of those in my line of work into alignment with global ecological realities?

✧ What would it take for my place of work to make the environment a key priority in its strategic planning?

✧ Will it be possible to motivate enough people to do what really needs to be done?

✧ What can I do to remember the physical environment in every decision I make?

FIVE

The Ever Receding Goal of Economic Development

"The prevailing "master plan" operating around the planet today is to go on consuming until there is nothing left to consume."

DANIEL QUINN, *ISHMAEL*

"Very little of "First World" development in the "Third World," and even less of business investment, has been at all beneficial to the vast majority of the "Third World's" people."

HERMAN DALY

"All industrial nations are rapidly consuming our capital assets (natural resources) and counting it on the profit side of the ledger. A basic tenet of capitalism is that you do not consume capital to pay for current expenses. Businesses that do, go bankrupt. We are managing our planet as if it were a business in liquidation."

GAYLORD NELSON

Most, if not all, of the economics models that are in widespread use today were developed at a time when nearly all financial transactions were carried out within any given country's borders. The scale of human activity was such that the models didn't have to account for long term adverse environmental or resource depletion effects. Therefore, these "costs" are left out of pricing policies. Economists assume that the air and water are free, that resources will always be available, that pollution adds no cost, and that industrial growth is the only viable means of development. Ultimately, all economic activity is necessarily dependent on the availability of natural resources.

Today, there is no such thing as a domestic economy, and it is becoming clear that our sense of progress in the West is based on the unvoiced assumption that we'll never have enough. Extending our western patterns of consumption to the rest of the world would obviously be devastating; conversely, widening the gap between the "haves" and "have nots," as we are now doing, will eventually lead to massive conflicts. So, we must soon answer the question "How far can the global economy continue to expand without irreversible environmental and social repercussions that will undermine quality of life?"

Changes in our natural systems caused by human activity will, by definition, eventually have profound economic significance. Biological organisms have a limited capacity to resist variations in climate and the presence of toxins. The capacities of air, water, and soil to assimilate wastes are also limited.

The still prevalent response is to ignore these growing pressures and try ever harder to make our financial systems provide us with healthy returns. It is a little bit like going to the doctor and asking for a quick healing, but begging the doctor to not make us give up any of our unhealthy habits. Along the same lines, while a growing proportion of the population is now admitting that present human activities are unsustainable, most of us still don't want to let go of our attachments to economic growth, unlimited resource consumption, return on investment, the free dumping of visible and molecular waste, and the valuation of people as a function of their usefulness to the economy.

If we are to think systemically, as the latest business and management literature says we must, then we must seek the underlying conditions for which today's economic, environmental, and social challenges are the symptoms. If we don't address these underlying conditions, once they are identified they will continue to generate additional, presumably more severe, challenges and pressures. The nature of economics models suggests that there is no reason to believe that economic logic will lead to sound social decisions or decisions that make systemic sense. Rather, present economic decisions are made to maximize short run return, and since future generations don't contribute to the short term return rate, they have no value in economic logic.

This chapter on economics and sustainability is divided into six sections: The history of money; The rise of speculation; The problem of interest; The costs of doing business; The ever receding goal of economic development; and Some hopeful signs.

The History of Money[6]

Money as we know it today probably came into being around 2000 BCE. This was not beads or shells, but money that satisfied three criteria: it could be subdivided into standardized units of value (like dollars, quarters, dimes, etc.); it was a medium of exchange (it could be spent or lent); and it was a store of value (it contained a fixed amount of "buying power").

As far as we know, this money first appeared in ancient Sumer. Farmers, who made up most of the population, were required to pay taxes to the temples, at a set percentage of the amount of barley they grew. Thus, the grain harvests directly supported the priests and the royal family. Barley units were used to pay for building construction and for various commodities. They were also stockpiled to provide food during times of drought. In this way, the ancient Sumerian priests served also as bankers.

---

[6] The sections entitled "The History of Money" and "The Rise of Speculation" are strongly influenced by Joel Kurtzman's *The Death of Money*.

The unit of barley was called a "Shay." These shays stored value, were spendable, and could be divided into standardized "sub-shays." At some point, the priests hit on an idea. Rather than giving out actual barley shays to pay for things, they decided to give out something symbolic of the barley instead — something easier to carry around; something that could be redeemed for a set amount of barley at the temple, if desired. They used a specific sized piece of bronze to represent the value of a shay of barley. This equivalent unit became the first "modern" money and was called the "shay-kel" or shekel, a term which is still used for the monetary unit in Israel.

Eventually these pieces of bronze were stamped into disks, and even had pictures of the barley they represented imprinted on them. Later, images of the ruler and/or of the prevailing deity were added to these coins. The priests also made coins out of silver and gold, and each of the money pieces had a fixed value relative to the shekel. With these innovations, ancient Sumer was on the "barley standard." The word spread rapidly, and within a few centuries most countries had adopted coinage with the same properties as the Sumerians had created.

For 4000 years, money has continued in much the same form. One change was that coins came to be backed by quantities of silver or gold rather than barley. A second change, made about 2000 years ago by the Chinese, was to use paper as a cheaper way to symbolize an amount of gold.

Otherwise, money stayed pretty much the same until August 15, 1972, when then president Nixon took to the airwaves to announce his plans for fixing an "ailing" economy. He placed a 10% surcharge on Japanese imports, froze wages and prices, restricted strikes, and took the U.S. dollar off the gold standard. The surtax on Japanese imports lasted less than a year. The wage and price controls and the restriction on strikes got most of the press attention — these lasted 90 days. The removal of the dollar from the gold standard, and allowing it to "float" relative to other currencies, received very little attention from the media. Nixon, in effect, abolished a 4000-year-old monetary system.

Up to that point, the dollar was the "modern" world's reserve currency. Most other countries insured the value of their currencies by holding the gold backed dollar in their reserve banks.After Nixon's announcement, the World's currencies began to fluctuate in value. At the time, about $100 billion were held abroad as a result of U.S. spending on the Viet Nam War and the financing of military bases in Europe and Asia. When these dollars were set free of ties to gold held in the U.S., their value began to fluctuate and they formed the basis for an unregulated global dollar economy. With the value of these dollars up for grabs, speculators could make a quick fortune by buying dollars when they were cheap and selling them when their value rose.

Throughout the seventies and eighties, the prices of real estate, oil, gold, silver and other commodities fluctuated wildly. Coincidentally, computers came into widespread use at this same time. Rapid fluctuations in value, plus the instantaneous transactions made possible by a global network of computers, put speculation into high gear, and soon most of the money on the planet was involved with speculation rather than in paying for goods and services.

The Rise of Speculation

Ultimately, the health of our current global economy depends heavily on the continued success of speculators, and very little on the production of goods and services. Shortly after the value of the dollar began to fluctuate in value, traders recognized that changing values means an opportunity to make a profit, and a dollar trading pit was opened at the Chicago Mercantile Exchange in 1973. Today, all of the major trading centers around the world buy and sell dollars and other currencies with the sole purpose of making a profit from the changing relative values of money.

On an average day, over $800 billion dollars changes hands, mostly electronically, in these speculations. Only about $25 billion changes hands each days for goods and services, such as buying airplanes and computers and cars and having your house painted. This means that for every dollar spent on work and production, $32 is being spent in speculation. Put another way, New York, with its stock exchange, trading houses and banks, processes 1.3 trillion speculative dollars a day. Every three days, the equivalent of the U.S. annual gross domestic product passes through New York electronically. Every three weeks, the equivalent of the annual gross world product passes through New York!

The somewhat troubling result of these emerging conditions is that a few thousand people sitting at their computers around the world are deciding the value of any given currency, and hence the value of an hour of your work, in nanosecond time frames, without any consideration whatsoever of long term implications or planning.

The Problem of Interest[7]

In most parts of the world today, few people would question the assumption that the lender of money should receive interest. It seems completely sensible that one should expect a reasonable return if one lends money to others. Over the last few decades, and especially since the dollar was released from the gold standard, how much interest is seen as reasonable has increased dramatically.

Historically, the term "usury" has been used to indicate profiteering from lending money and charging large amounts to the borrower for access to the money. The term "interest" once meant the amount of just compensation that could be expected for losses associated with lending money. Usury has been unacceptable, down through the ages. It is denounced in the Bible and the Koran, and by Greece, Rome, Thomas Aquinas, Martin Luther, and Gandhi.

Contemporary business operates with interest rates that would

---

[7] The section entitled "The Problem of Interest" is strongly influenced by Willis Harman (1992 and 1994).

have been condemned as usurious just a few decades ago. Debt, gambling, and speculation have rapidly become a way of life. In the '90s, between 30-50% of every dollar a household spends goes into mostly hidden debt servicing. It has been predicted that since personal debt levels are so high and savings levels are so low, most people in the U.S. will outlive their assets!

The effect of high rates of interest is to shift steadily the location of money from the less wealthy to the more wealthy, as presumably the more wealthy have excess funds that can be lent, and the less wealthy need to borrow funds to carry on their enterprises. The borrowers then transfer wealth to the lenders when they repay the principle plus the high interest charges. The same thing is happening between the wealthier and poorer countries.

The result is that the rate of debt is increasing at around 10% a year worldwide (that is, the total indebtedness in the world is doubling approximately every seven years). All but a very few people spend far more on interest every year than they earn in interest. One unfortunate result is that developing countries everywhere are being forced to give away their natural resources to pay the interest on their debts.

As the amount of debt increases relative to the amount of income, governments are pressured to print more money which, of course, engenders inflation. In essence, we borrow money into existence, watering down the real value of each unit. Today, banks regularly create money in the form of credit equal to many times their actual reserves. Since most of the money in existence today has been borrowed into existence, it is impossible to ever repay all the interest that has been charged — that would mean repaying more money than *actually* exists!

In turn, this leads to the need for continuous speculation, so that as we saw in the previous section, less than 5% of the total daily financial flow is for goods and services — the rest is pure speculation. One highly profitable form of speculation is the production of arms, which can be maintained as long as we can maintain the mental imagery of threatening enemies, of "Us vs. Them."

In summary, the cash surplus of the wealthy flows around the world electronically seeking the best investment and speculation opportunities available to make even more money. Unfortunately the rates of return on most environmentally friendly or ecologically desirable opportunities aren't high enough to attract much of this money. Even agriculture is financed by short term return on investment interests, with little or no concern for the long term viability of the top soil which, as a consequence is being rapidly lost in most agricultural areas of the planet. There is a huge world wide economic momentum that revolves around those with surplus cash increasing their wealth (often at the expense of the less wealthy) with speculative investments that lead to quick payoffs. One has to wonder whether we have the will, or the means, collectively, to reinvent our economic system.

The present system, as inequitable as it is, was made up in the human mind, so there is at least the potential to make up another one that works better for the "other 99%" of the population!

> Four (and a half) decades of post World War II economic development have left at least a billion people in dire poverty and most of the developing world in economic difficulty. It has *created* enormous economic disparities between rich and poor (such that the average American uses as much energy as 20 Indians) without abating in the slightest the pressures for further economic growth in the most affluent countries. . .   The most affluent countries currently receive net resource outflows from the less developed of $50 billion per year — the amount of Egypt's total gross national product. (Repeto, 1990, p.72).

The Costs of Doing Business

One of the quotes at the beginning of this chapter, by Gaylord Nelson, points out that consuming our capital assets without paying for them is a surefire road to bankruptcy. This is just what we are doing on a global scale. In our industrial accounting processes, we do not consider the costs of: minerals extracted, top soil lost, inadequately treated waste, fish removed from the ocean, declining biodiversity, and so on. Under the prevailing economic models, these are free resources that should (even *must*) be exploited to create immediate wealth for shareholders (many of whom are the same senior executives of the companies who preach shareholder return as sacrosanct).

The same is true of the manufacturing process itself. There usually is no cost charged to the consumer of toxic compounds released into the waterways or greenhouse gasses released into the atmosphere, unless required by the government. In fact the government's "pollution credits" can be bought and sold almost like commodities. In many cases, it is cheaper to purchase another company's pollution quota than it is to clean up one's own manufacturing process. So long as the net effect on the environment is "acceptable" to the government regulators, they don't care who does the polluting. In fact, pollution clean-up counts positively in the way we calculate Gross Domestic Product, so there are certain forces within our economic system that do not want to see us ending our polluting ways!

Harold M. Hubbard (1991), writing for *Scientific American*, estimated that the cost to the U.S. of the Gulf War would add $23.50 to each barrel of oil imported for a several year period. Since our government subsidizes the price of oil, individuals and corporations who buy oil based products are not paying the full cost, just as we are not asked to pay anything for the relative depletion of our global oil reserves.

As with *all* products made from extracted raw materials, we are asked to pay far less than the true cost of creating them. Minimizing the costs we pay for energy and for other goods will create many pressures over the decades to come. As the global population grows, the demands for consumer products and for energy will also grow steeply in developing countries, as the people there strive to raise their living standards and to adopt the consumer life style of the West.

To speed the process of "catching up" with the developed countries, and to generate cash to pay off huge interest payments on past debts, many developing countries are selling off vast tracts of forest lands to Japanese and North American timber interests. As a result, clear cutting of forests is being carried out on a massive scale in Russia and Surinam. India has sold fishing rights in its coastal waters for cash, jeopardizing the livelihoods of its own 7.5 million fishermen. Libya is tapping a huge aquifer which underlies the country, in an attempt to turn their desert nation into an instant vegetable garden, in what amounts to the largest civil engineering project in the history of mankind, with little or no attention to what it will do when the aquifer is depleted.

The full costs of modern consumerism are difficult to quantify accurately. In addition to the costs implied in these examples, we must also consider the long term health effects of pollution; the life time costs of major energy related accidents such as Chernobyl, the Valdez oil spill, tanker truck fires on freeways, and Three Mile island; the generation and release of greenhouse gasses and ozone layer depleting gasses; the effects of habitat destruction; the costs of topsoil loss and increased desertification; and the dislocations of people caused by major up and down cycles in local economies.

Since the end of WW II, the global population has more than doubled, but our global economic production has grown five fold, with no sign of slowing down. We can reasonably expect another five fold increase in production in the next fifty years — can we afford to delay paying attention to the true costs of this productivity until we are *sure* what they are?

Today, it is economic decisions alone, NOT God or natural selection, which determine which animals and plants will inhabit the earth. Species that survive under today's "rules" will do so only if they have more *economic* value alive than not alive. The goals of economic growth in the short term and an environment that is sustainable in the long term are by definition in conflict.

The Ever Receding Goal of Economic Development

The avowed goal of the original developers of modern economic theories and models was to provide a means for furthering *human development*. It is appropriate to check into how we are doing on this set of goals as we draw this chapter to a close. Has economic activity actually promoted human welfare in the less developed parts of the world? Are poorer people catching up with the wealthier people in the more developed countries?

The available results don't look very encouraging at all. Rather, they point to a trend, both among individuals and among countries, that the rich are continuing to get richer and the poor are continuing to get poorer in comparison.

According to *Business Week* (1992), within 35 years the global population will be approximately 11 billion, barring a major calamity. Most of the people born over the next 35 years will live in developing nations, where the poor are already forced to destroy their habitats just to stay alive. The income disparity of the top 20% of nations and the bottom 20% has shifted dramatically over the last 35 years, and there seems to be no reason to think that this trend will change. In 1960, the average income per capita in the top fifth of countries was 30 times that of the per capita income of those in the bottom fifth. Each decade the disparity has increased: 32-1 in 1970; 45-1 in 1980; and 59-1 in 1990!

Even within the wealthy countries, the gap between rich and poor is widening. A research study initiated in Luxembourg found that the gap between rich and poor families with children in the U.S. is the largest among the top 18 industrial countries (*San Francisco Chronicle*, August 15, 1995, p 2). Among the countries studied, poor American families were the poorest except for those in Ireland and Israel. Rich American families were the richest, averaging $6000 per family of four more than families in second place Switzerland.

These findings were essentially duplicated in a survey conducted by the Organization for Economic Cooperation and Development

(OECD) headquartered in Paris (*San Francisco Chronicle*, October 28, 1995). Their survey compared those in the top 10% in income with those in the bottom 10%. The United States has the largest gap, with the richest people earning 59 times as much as the poorest. The U.S. was followed by Ireland, Italy, Canada, Australia and Great Britain (where the gap is presently growing the fastest). Thus, with the exception of Ireland, those countries with the widest gaps between rich an poor are among the most economically "developed" in the world!

Another study, reported in *Business Week* (1993), reported that the CEOs of the largest U.S. corporations earned 42 times as much as the lowest paid workers in those companies in 1970; and 157 times as much in 1990. By 1997, they were earning 200 times as much! Clearly a small percent of the population at large is reaping the benefits of today's economic activity. The big question is "How much longer can this go on, before the masses of people who are losing ground refuse to put up with any further decline in their relative affluence?"

Only seven countries account for half of the greenhouse gases generated by human activity today. As the developing countries attempt to industrialize, we can expect that the worldwide emissions of greenhouse gases will leap upward.

Those 25% of the people alive today who live in already industrialized nations are consuming 70% of the resources being used in manufacturing. As the developing countries attempt to catch up, we can expect that the demand for natural resources will also leap upward. Further, in 1989, developing countries owed an average of 44% of their collective Gross Domestic Product in debt. As a result, there are tremendous pressures, as already noted, for them to sell off their natural resources for quick cash, rather than using those resources themselves to create value added production which would allow for progress towards self sufficiency.

Some Hopeful Signs

All the indicators are not negative, however, as a growing number of people are beginning to enquire into the trends reported in this chapter. Further, more and more people are concluding that an "activity-focused" life that has as its goal the acquisition of material goods, is much less rewarding than a more "being focused" life that has as its goal self realization and fulfillment (Russell, 1995).

Harvard economist Juliet Schor (1991) points out that in the U.S., the average worker is now working at least 162 hours a year more than in 1970 — about a full month's work per year more than a couple of decades ago. The total work year in America often entails an extra two months' worth of work per year more than in Europe. The logical conclusion of the "doing/having" mindset is clearly that we should therefore be happier than we were in 1970.

But are we? One study, reported in *The Futurist* magazine in 1993, asked this question and found out that on average, people in the U.S. are no more or less happy than they were in the early 1950s, when each person worked far less than today's average number of hours, and consumed about half as many goods and services as the average person consumes today. In both cases, about 30% of the population at each level of income report that they are reasonably to fully satisfied with their lives.

This leads to the question of "What *are* the major contributors to happiness and fulfillment?" Research into the strongest contributors to happiness and fulfillment have found that there is no correlation between "having" and "happiness." The strongest predictors of these elusive qualities appear to be: *meaningful* work, deep family and friend relationships, and opportunities to use one's true talents or capabilities. In short, "meaning and relationships" are far better predictors of fulfillment in life than "doing and having." Pete Russell's enquiries (1995), as reported in *The Global Brain Awakens*, suggest that the number of people who realize this is growing rapidly.

Alternative accounting procedures are being devised in many quarters, and talk of a dual, even treble, bottom line is increasing. Hazel Henderson (1978, 1988, and 1991) has argued widely and persuasively that we must create a Human Development Index to replace the Gross Domestic product measure. Her measure would include the following indices, in addition to monetary measures of societal health:

- ✧ Degree of personal freedom.
- ✧ Level of government inefficiency.
- ✧ Ratio of military to civilian expenditures.
- ✧ Level of relative poverty.
- ✧ Inventories of toxic and radioactive waste.
- ✧ Level of literacy.

The closing question of this chapter is "Is a smooth shift from primarily quantitative financial growth to more qualitative human growth possible?" There are many experiments underway today that are testing the ideas of alternative economic accounting. There are new forms of employee ownership being undertaken in many places around the world. There are also a growing number of communities that are exploring the possibilities of local forms of currency. A few of these are briefly summarized here.

As I pointed out near the beginning of this chapter, money as we know it today probably came into being around 2000 BCE, and satisfied three criteria: it could be subdivided into standardized units of value (like dollars, quarters, dimes, etc.); it was a medium of exchange (it could be spent or lent); and it was a store of value (it contained a fixed amount of "buying power"). For well over 3000 years, the common substance of money was most often some precious metal, such as gold or silver. As long as you knew the weight and fineness of the coin, you knew what it was worth.

A few hundred years ago, mostly as a matter of convenience, paper notes were introduced to represent the ownership of metal. The paper was easy to handle, and the metal it represented was stored safely away in a government vault. While there were some abuses, such as central banks that occasionally issued more paper money than there was precious metal to support it, the system worked pretty well. Since the dollar was removed from the gold standard in 1972, however, the major currencies of the world have added another characteristic. It also is now used as a tool for speculative profit.

While money today serves four or more purposes — subdivisible standard of measure, medium of exchange, store of value, and tool of speculation — it really only needs to serve two purposes. We need money that provides a standard measure, and we need money that provides a convenient medium of exchange.

The idea of creating local currencies that satisfy these two functions is not new. "Scrip" money was issued in hundreds of places during the depression of the 1930s, and functioned very effectively in local economies. One big success was the "Merchandise Bonds" issued by the Larkin Company in Buffalo, New York in 1933. These bonds were used by the company to pay its employees and could be used to purchase goods and services from any Larkin outlet in the country. Eventually, other businesses also began to accept the Larkin bonds. The company's accountants estimated that the original $36,000 issue of bonds were spent enough times that they generated the sale of $250,000 worth of merchandise and services, providing a significant boost to business during the depression.

The most widespread contemporary approach to a local currency is known as the LETS system, which originally stood for the Local Exchange Trading System, but soon became the Local Employment and Trading System. This system, known as a mutual credit system, was created in British Columbia, Canada in the early 1980s. LETS systems have proliferated rapidly, and there are hundreds operating in all parts of the world. In 1993, there were 10 in the U.S., 20 in Canada, 20 in Ireland, 120 in Great Britain, 60 in New Zealand, and 160 in Australia.

Michael Linton, the originator, created LETS as a not-for-profit membership association which operates in parallel with the monetary system. When members sell goods or services to another member, they receive credits. When they buy goods or services from another member they receive debits. This stimulates buying and selling within the local community and reduces dependency on the outside marketplace, while building community and mutual support. Each local LETS system is independent and can assign whatever value it likes to its LETS unit.

Perhaps the most successful and best known local currency plan within the United States is called *Ithaca Hours*, which was launched in Ithaca, New York, in late 1991 by Paul Glover. This popular system is based on "hours" being issued in exchange for advertising in a newsletter Glover publishes. These "hours" can then be spent for purchases from anyone willing to accept them. Glover has also developed a kit that describes how to set up the system. Hundreds of people all over the United States have bought these kits, and similar programs have begun to spring up in many places as a result.

To summarize this section, let me refer to the writing of Thomas Greco (1992, 1994), who has been writing about alternative money systems for several years. He has offered a prescription for an economically healthy community:[8]

   ◇ Organize a community of cooperators — people willing to work together for a better future for themselves and their children.

   ◇ Set standards for the quality of life you want and insist on reaching them.

   ◇ Build on *available* resources and abilities.

   ◇ Create buffering structures between global and local economies — in particular, a local currency similar to LETS.

   ◇ Maximize local value added.

   ◇ Spend locally, save locally, invest locally.

   ◇ Create a diversity of skills.

---

[8] I am indebted to Willis Harman for introducing me to Greco's work.

Questions For Contemplation And Dialogue

✧ Can I support making progress on the obvious global needs and challenges and still make a decent living?

✧ What will it take to catalyze people to live less greedily?

✧ How can we speak for the poor if we don't know any poor people?

✧ What would it take to build the environmental and depletion costs into our economic transactions instead of postponing them?

✧ When will we learn to measure organizational performance in more ways than just money?

✧ What would it take to reduce the income gaps between the rich few and the multitudes of poor people?

✧ What am I doing solely in order to "have" and to "maintain?"

✧ Are economic survival and spiritual growth possible together over the long haul?

✧ What has real value?

✧ Will I ever be able to feel secure in my work life again?

✧ Is what's happening to our planet part of a divine plan that we shouldn't be concerned about?

✧ What will we devise to replace solely quantitative growth?

Six

Global Crowding

"If the world's population had the productivity of the Swiss, the consumption habits of the Chinese, the egalitarian instincts of the Swedes, and the social discipline of the Japanese, then the planet could support several times its current population without privation for anyone. On the other hand, if the world's population had the productivity of Chad, the consumption habits of the United States, the inegalitarian instincts of India, and the social discipline of Argentina, then the planet could not support anywhere near its current numbers."

LESTER THUROW

"In 1968, there were 3.5 billion people on Earth and the population was growing by some 70 million per year. In 1991 the world had 5.4 billion people to support, not 3.5 billion; and the annual population increase was roughly 95 million, not 70 million."

PAUL EHRLICH

At the beginning of the "Common Era," (Year 0), it is estimated that there were approximately 300 million people alive on the Earth, slightly more people on the whole planet than presently inhabit the United

States. Over the next 1000 years, the population of the planet had only grown by 10 million. In 1500, there were approximately half a billion, and around 1800, the population finally reached a billion. By 1900, there were approximately 1.65 billion people living on the Earth. In the

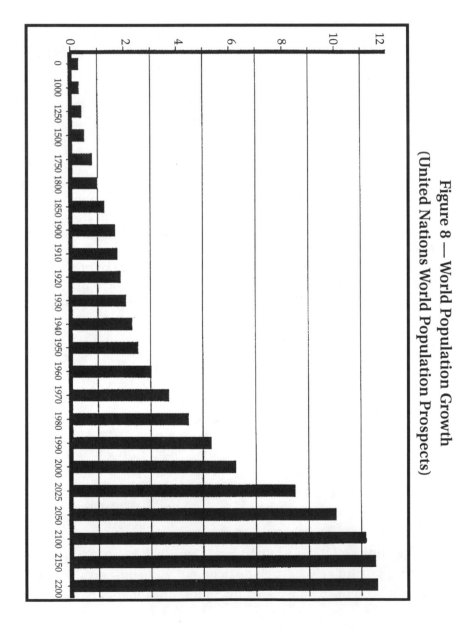

Figure 8 — World Population Growth
(United Nations World Population Prospects)

Figure 9 — World Population Growth in the 20th Century (United Nations World Population Prospects)

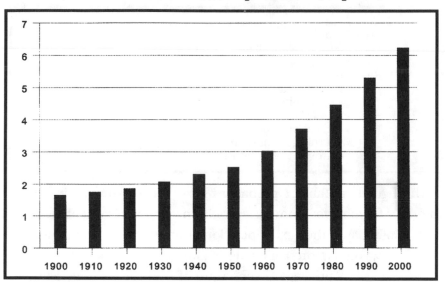

year 2000, barring major catastrophes, there will be over six billion. The global population has more than tripled in this century, and by most projections, will likely double again before finally leveling off sometime in the next 100 to 200 years.

Today's reality is that there are presently about six billion people living on the earth, and that around 80 million new people are added every year (i.e. approximately 9,000 per hour).

Most of today's prevailing economic models were developed when the global population was less than four billion, which we attained in the early 1970s. Most of today's leaders came of age and completed their formal educations when there were less than four billion people.

These numbers are so large that it is difficult for us to comprehend what they may mean, especially in relation to their complex interactions with the ecological and economic situations described in the preceding chapters. Another way to consider the population of the planet is to imagine that we could shrink the population of the Earth today to a village of 100 people, with all present ratios remaining the same. Here is how some of the demographics would appear.

Table 1
Global Demographics

57	Asians
21	Europeans
14	Western Hemisphere
8	Africans
70	non-white, 30 white
70	unable to read
80	living in substandard housing or homeless
70	non-Christian
50	with malnutrition
1	with college education
6	control 50% of world wealth

The figures in Table 1 probably place you, the reader, in a tiny minority, far removed from the everyday pressures of most of the population of today. If the next population doubling occurs in the next 30 or so years, your children and grandchildren may not be able to identify with such a "privileged" sub group of the global family as most readers of this book can today.

As in the cases of ecology and economics, there are those who contend that there is nothing to be concerned about relative to supporting such a large population. They generally base their arguments on how well we are doing TODAY, rightfully pointing out that most malnutrition today is due to political restrictions on distribution of food, rather than on our ability to produce enough food. They generally do not address our ability to do so when the population doubles again. Their arguments also tend NOT to address the drastic loss of topsoil and the severe degradation of our water supplies that have taken place during the 1900s. Rather they focus on "unproven" effects such as global warming or the ozone "hole." They state that these conditions aren't proven, and therefore imply that they are not real.

In reviewing both the arguments predicting near future difficulties arising from global warming and the thinning of the ozone layer *and* those denying that these processes are even happening, I personally find the former to be more compelling, more scientific, and more data based; and the latter to be more strident and seemingly more politically motivated. As I wrote earlier in this book, I am operating from the assumption that it is not too early, and hopefully not too late, to adopt a more preventive orientation to the probable challenges of the future.

Those who argue for ignoring the rate of population growth frequently cite the high density living arrangements in places like the U.S. state of New Jersey, Switzerland, and The Netherlands which each provide high quality of life for a large percentage of their inhabitants. They almost never, however, mention that none of these places is self sufficient in food, and that water supply and air and water quality are constant problems.

Granted, all of the people on the earth today *could* be crammed into an area the size of Texas, leaving the rest of the world for food production, parks, and animal preserves. None of these advocates' articles that I have read, nor any I have talked to, have any kind of plan for how to convince everyone to move into such an arrangement!

A further gap in my understanding of these arguments for ignoring population growth, or even encouraging it, is how to consider the drain on the natural resources required to supply food, energy, and material goods. Also ignored are how the rising expectations will be met for a material world fostered in the far corners of the earth by globalized media coverage of the consumption today in the developed West. And no one, to my knowledge, has proposed a workable process for recycling or disposing of the waste products of such a vast consumer society. Although, to be fair, one supporter of unbridled population growth has recently suggested that our "landfills" could be made much taller than they are now. Trash mountains?

It appears to me that we humans have undertaken a number of simultaneous experiments, such as rapidly releasing vast amounts of carbon dioxide and chlorinated compounds into the environment, rapidly adding people to our ranks, allowing the loss of huge amounts of topsoil each year (four and a half metric tons per person per year are presently being washed away — 25 billion metric tons worldwide), allowing our fresh water supplies to be degraded, and so on. Since we have never tried these experiments before on a global scale, we have no way of knowing for sure what the results will be of their combined effects. Astoundingly to me, many very intelligent people argue that we should continue these experiments indefinitely, until we are "sure" that they are bad for us.

An additional factor that seems to be fueling the pressure on the planetary systems is the globalization of the media. People in the remotest villages of the economically poorest countries in the world now have access to TVs with satellite offerings such as MTV from Tokyo, 24-hour news from the BBC, and soap operas from the US. The images of material "success" beamed to these remote corners of the earth are having a strong effect on the expectations of people around the world. "Why can't we have these things too?" is the perfectly reasonable response.

The overall population growth rate is negative among "affluent" people, defined as those who have discretionary income (who make up 6% of the total population, and control half of the total wealth); and the "middle classes," defined as those who are making ends meet (9% of the total) around the world. The population is still growing among those who are at the impoverished end of the economic scale or essentially exist outside of the economic realm (85% of the total). Increasingly, those who are in the still growing 85% of the population are making it known that they expect to have the material comforts enjoyed today by the relatively wealthy 15%. This, of course, is placing heavy demands on natural resources, waste disposal, and air and water qualities. Beijing, for example, suffers today from appalling air quality. Cleaning it up is of much less economic importance than is continued rapid growth in production, and therefore supply, of goods for the masses.

Prior to these rising expectations, many "poor" people were living sustainable life styles. There is, I believe, significant doubt that the life styles they are now learning to aspire to are anywhere near as sustainable.

While expectations for material goods like we have in North America, Europe, Japan, Australia, and New Zealand are rising in the emerging nations, utopians are forecasting a Golden Age of high tech material affluence. They seem to base their projections on tomorrow's technology breakthroughs, but apparently with the global population of 1900 in their minds. If we think back to the numbers and the life styles and the pace of changes of 100 years ago and compare them with today, how can we even begin to conceive of the challenges and opportunities of 100 years from now?

For example, one of the effects of modernizing India's agricultural practices to bring that country to food self sufficiency was to put millions of small plot farmers out of work. With no way to carry on with the only life they knew, these millions have migrated into the cities of India in search of work, and have overburdened the infrastructures of Bombay, Calcutta, Delhi and Bangalore.

Likewise, political, ecological, and economic conditions around the world have set millions of people into motion as refugees, looking for a better life away from the places of their birth. While these waves of mass migration are apparently only beginning, more and more of the so called advanced countries are already moving to close their borders.

Some Implications

In the lexicon of meteorologists, a "tornado watch" means that the conditions are right for a tornado. A "tornado alert" means that a tornado has been sighted. I want to use the "watch" metaphor to take the slightly more conservative road in making some of the trends and implications more detailed.

CHINAWATCH: China, it is predicted, will soon surpass the U.S. and Japan as the largest user of steel, which will cause a scramble for this metal. It will surpass the U.S. in energy consumption and become another net oil importer by the turn of the century. It is likely that by the year 2025, China will be releasing three times as much carbon dioxide into the atmosphere as the U.S. In fact, China is already the third largest contributor of greenhouse gases; but because of its size and population, it today does not rank in the top 50 of "per capita"

emitters of greenhouse gases. While the economically developed countries are taking steps to curb their greenhouse gas emissions, China is
not showing any signs of sacrificing any of its economic growth for the
sake of its own environment or the world's. (Minkin, 1995).

MIGRATIONWATCH: Tens of millions of people are migrating all over
the world in search of a safer way of life, or for work, or for improved
living conditions. Many are today looking to the economically developed and relatively underpopulated areas of North America as the
place they want to migrate to. Within the U.S. there are also migration
patterns away from the northeast and towards the south and southwest. Let's look into the changes taking place today in the "sun belt" of
the U.S., where the population is growing very rapidly due to
increased births, longer life expectancies, and high levels of migration.

In the last few years, the U.S. has accepted more immigrants than all
other industrialized nations combined. Large portions of these new-
comers have settled in the U.S. south and southwest.
Underemployment in the economically developing nations will continue to fuel the migration to the U.S. for the foreseeable future. By
2015, it is estimated (Minkin, 1995) that half of all population growth
in the U.S. Sunbelt will be due to immigration. As a result, today the
Asian American population is growing eight times faster than that of
European Americans; and the Hispanic population is growing four
times faster than the European Americans.

Clearly, heretofore unknown levels of tolerance for diversity will be
needed. Pressure on clean water supplies will be enormous, and most
food and other goods will have to be brought in from other regions.

These same dynamics are happening in many parts of the world.
When they run into another contemporary set of dynamics — funda-
mentalism and ethnic purity — the potential for worldwide strife
seems quite high.

URBANWATCH: UrbanWatch is a subset of MigrationWatch, as most
of the rapid growth of our cities is driven by people coming to them
from rural areas. For the most part, these migrants to the cities bring

few skills usable in city life and work, but come seeking work and the "good life" of running water, flush toilets, air conditioners, and TVs. Since the migrants usually don't add significant wealth to the cities of their choice, the tax base soon becomes inadequate, resulting in declines in the quality of the schools and the infrastructure of the cities, and contributing further to a vicious cycle of congestion, pollution, poor sanitation, decaying roads and bridges, and lowered literacy rates.

Many Asian cities today are degrading at a much faster rate than their growing national economies can keep up with. It has been estimated that by 2020, an additional one and a half billion people will be living in the cities of Asia compared to today. This trend is happening all around the world, with the highest rates of population growth occurring in the cities of the economically less well off countries. The table below shows the world's largest cities in 1994, and projects the changes in megacity populations in just two decades — to 2015.

FOODWATCH: Up until about 1985, food production pretty well kept up with the growth in global population, even though political factors inhibited distribution to all areas of concentrated population. Since 1985, however, food production has been declining as the population

Table 2
Projected Global Urbanization

POPULATION OF THE WORLD'S LARGEST CITIES (Millions)			
1994		**2015**	
Tokyo	26.8	Tokyo	28.7
Sao Paulo	16.4	Bombay	27.4
New York	16.3	Lagos	24.4
Mexico City	15.6	Shanghai	23.4
Bombay	15.1	Jakarta	21.2
Shanghai	15.1	Sao Paulo	20.8
Los Angeles	12.4	Karachi	20.6
Beijing	12.4	Beijing	19.4
Calcutta	11.7	Dhaka	19.0
Seoul	11.6	Mexico City	18.8

Source: Associated Press

has continued to grow — especially in Latin America and Africa. Grain production has been declining gradually, while fisheries production is markedly diminished. Humans have over-fished and polluted the seas, and destroyed vast tracts of wetlands that serve as nurseries for many species.

Climate changes also hurt food production. Whether or not they are indications of global warming, the more extreme weather of the past few years (droughts and storms) have severely curtailed food production. If global warming is a real phenomenon, then crops will have to be grown further to the north in the northern hemisphere and further to the south in the southern hemisphere. There is no certainty that our traditional crops, like corn and wheat, will grow as readily in the soils nearer the poles.

Desertification is promoted by climate change and by shortsighted agricultural methods. Between 1945 and 1990, a period of only 45 years, over three billion acres became nonarable — roughly the size of India and China combined, mostly due to weather changes and farming methods. As aquifers (underground water reservoirs) are drawn down, the water tends to have a higher salt content. Today, over 200 million agricultural acres around the world have salty soil to a significant degree, and the total is increasing rapidly.

The removal of the rain forests for the purposes of development and agriculture have been widely argued to be very short sighted. Not only are the rain forests the primary "lungs" of the earth, but their loss also heralds the loss of many species found only in the rainforests, which means a reduction in our planet's biodiversity, which is thought to be essential for the well-being of all species.

Further, the soil underlying these rainforests is generally quite poor, able to support crops for only a few years. When these forests are gone, the weather in these regions changes from wet to dry and new deserts emerge.

The role of women is seen more and more widely as being key to global sustainability as regards population. In the absence of economic involvement of women and when there is illiteracy, women tend to have far more children. Voluntary reductions in birth rate seem to follow quite naturally when female literacy rates and female participation in the economy increase. Beyond this, few viable solutions to the growth of the global population have been proposed that are humane and acceptable.

In closing this chapter, I want to cite a 1993 warning that was signed by 1700 scientists worldwide (including half of all living Nobel Laureates) and sponsored by 58 national Academies of Science:

> The earth is finite. Its ability to provide for growing numbers of people is finite, and we are fast approaching many of the earth's limits. Current economic practices, which damage the environment in both developed and underdeveloped nations, cannot be continued without the risk that global systems will be damaged beyond repair. Pressures resulting from unrestrained population growth put demands on the natural world that can overwhelm any efforts to achieve a sustainable future. If we are to halt the destruction of our environment, we must accept limits to that growth... Acting on this recognition is not altruism, but enlightened self interest, whether we are industrialized or not. We all have but one life boat. (Ehrlich, 1995).

Questions For Contemplation And Dialogue

✧ What, if anything, can/should we do about population growth?

✧ How much longer will we be able to feed everyone as the population grows and net farm production declines?

✧ What is the maximum population the earth can sustain — for centuries and centuries — at a decent standard of living?

✧ Of what use are the poor in the emerging world economic order?

- ✧ Is 70% of the global population "hopelessly poor" or are 6% of us hopelessly rich?

- ✧ To what extent is it even possible to achieve fair and equitable distribution of goods and services?

- ✧ How can the more and less economically developed parts of the world find common purpose and common goals?

- ✧ How can we foster stronger values of collaboration and cooperation within and across cultures? Should we value this?

- ✧ What is the cost of sharing resources equitably? What is the eventual cost of NOT sharing resources equitably?

- ✧ Who's going to change first?

- ✧ Can we ever expect to live "in community" on a global level?

- ✧ What do other countries know that we should be learning?

- ✧ If all my neighbors acted as I act, would we all be finding peace and joy?

- ✧ How can we ever expect anything to get better as long as we continue to do what we do to ourselves and our neighbors?

- ✧ How can we make more conscious connections between global challenges and local actions?

SECTION III

From Autopilot to Choice

IF WE CONTINUE TO BELIEVE AS WE HAVE ALWAYS BELIEVED, WE WILL CONTINUE to act as we have always acted. If we continue to act as we have always acted, we will continue to get what we have always gotten. It is clear that our beliefs and our values drive our behaviors. What is often less clear is what those beliefs and values actually are. Most of the time we are acting from an "autopilot" mode of consciousness. As Helmstetter (1986) and others have pointed out, we have several thousand thoughts a day, and probably about 95% of those thoughts are the same every day.

This repetitious thinking represents a tremendous reinforcement of the status quo. If we actually do choose to have a different future, we must first become aware of how our present beliefs and values are actually largely responsible for creating our every day experiences. Then, we have the ability to change how we are thinking, how we are behaving, and ultimately, the experiences we can expect to have.

Whenever the pressure on people increases, it is perfectly normal for them to move to more extreme versions of the beliefs they hold. Those with a conservative political viewpoint can be expected to become more conservative, those with a liberal viewpoint, more liberal. People who have a strong faith in God will move deeper into their spiritual beliefs, while many of those who don't believe there is any God will move more deeply into materialism or hedonism.

We can see the results of this all around us today. Unprecedented numbers of people are espousing extreme fundamentalist spiritual views, which hold that God expresses *Himself* only through this or that "messiah," and that salvation comes only from wholeheartedly accepting that messiah's teachings. Unprecedented numbers are also being drawn towards the "new thought" spiritual movements that believe the divinity is everywhere at all times and expresses itself through each and every one of us.

Senior executives, performers, and professional athletes in all sports, especially in the United States, are demanding and receiving ever more astronomical financial rewards. Those in less affluent groups are apparently about evenly divided between whether this concentration of wealth in a very few is a great thing or a horrible, greedy thing.

By the same token, some "experts" are proclaiming loudly that there is no challenge on the horizon. Other "experts" are proclaiming equally loudly that life on Earth will cease, or will be severely degraded, if massive changes are not made within the next thirty years in how we conduct ourselves in matters of business, agriculture, and reproduction.

This book, of course, is taking the position that those who are foreseeing challenges need to be listened to. If there are no significant challenges on the horizon (that is, we can use technology to address any ecological imbalances; we will be able to produce enough food indefinitely; we can go on forever withdrawing from an infinite supply of natural resources; and there are no limits to the number of people the planet can support), then we need not be concerned. However, on the off chance that our future might not be quite so rosy, I want to raise again the question of whether or not it will ever be appropriate to take a more preventive stance towards these kinds of challenges. If this is tenable, then my question becomes "When is the latest moment at which we can adopt such a stance and still maintain a high quality of life for an acceptable percentage of the population?"

We know from systems science that the consequences of some actions cannot be known for a relatively long period of time. For example, over half of the ozone depleting compounds that have escaped into the atmosphere have not yet reached the ozone layer, and each year we learn that the "ozone hole" is bigger than the year before. Skin cancer rates are already skyrocketing everywhere on earth, and we have no way of knowing what the eventual quality of the ozone layer will be. Yet since a few scientists tell us that there isn't really a danger, and since it is still in the short term self interests of some constituencies to continue using and losing these compounds, and since the magnitude of the potential challenge is not part of our everyday awareness, we hold on to the expectation that somehow the ozone layer problem will just go away.

In the first chapter, I began by citing Ronald Laing's assertion that the difficulty with making fundamental changes is that "We fail to notice that we fail to notice." The result of this ever-so-normal human process is that when we are in the autopilot mode of thinking and behaving, which for most everyone is most of the time, we unwittingly operate in ways to protect the status quo. The two chapters in this section are intended to help us move to a more conscious, more choiceful, state of consciousness.

Questions For Contemplation And Dialogue

- ✧ What mechanisms can be created to examine our status quo collusions which are impeding change?
- ✧ Are there dangers in changing?
- ✧ How do we find the courage to express our views and feelings in environments that don't want to hear them?
- ✧ Can we learn to challenge the prevailing definitions of growth and success?
- ✧ What level of challenge will it take for me to truly and permanently change?

❖ What are the consequences of *not* changing my behavior?

❖ What fears must I deal with to unblock the path forward?

❖ How can I interrupt my daily autopilot activities in order to develop needed new habits of thinking and acting?

❖ What can I do to heighten my intention to change — how can I become passionately committed to changes that I discover are needed?

❖ What will it take for me to sustain the "big picture" when that picture paralyzes me?

❖ Am I really living what I know to be true?

SEVEN

Somebody Ought To Do Something About That

"There are no human passengers on spaceship Earth; every-one is crew."

BUCKMINSTER FULLER

"Never doubt for a moment that a small group of dedicated citizens can change the world. Indeed, it's the only thing that ever has."

MARGARET MEAD

"Nobody has ever made a greater mistake than those who do nothing because they feel they can do only a little."

EDMUND BURKE

As described in Chapter 3, all through history the dominant institution in society has taken responsibility for its sphere of influence. Up until 400 years ago in the "Western world," the church was the dominant institution. Then with the 17th century paradigm shift, gradually the state took over. As you will probably know from history class, we gave the church the "intangibles" like the human spirit, and the national governments eventually became the dominant institution for everything "real," and took responsibility for their realms of influence.

And today, financial enterprise has become the dominant institution all over the world. The church took responsibility when it was dominant; the state took responsibility when it was dominant, and now there is really nobody taking responsibility for the whole, which is now the whole eco-system of the planet.

In order to understand what it means to take responsibility, I'd like to introduce *"somebody,"* as in the "somebody at your house and mine who left the lights on, or ate the last of the yogurt; the somebody who ought to clean out the garage!"

I was once involved in helping a large organization develop a strategic plan. Throughout that organization, people were often heard to say "Somebody ought to do something about that!" As one example, they had a food service that no one cared for very much. It would have taken only one person to go and talk to the manager of the cafeteria about making some healthier and tastier options available, but no one ever did. It was always "Somebody ought to do something about that lousy food!" After a period of working with the top team, I found that they all recognized that "Somebody ought to do something about that" was an element of their culture that they wanted to change.

At the end of the strategic planning activity, I took the flip chart sheets with the follow up action items and accountabilities down off the wall and asked "Who is going to take these sheets and get them copied and distributed?" Everyone of the top executives looked down at the floor, waiting for "somebody" to volunteer. When "somebody" didn't show up, I gave the sheets to the CEO, which he took without saying anything. Of course, nothing ever happened with the strategic plan. I found out a little later that the CEO was upset with me for asking him to find "somebody."

Another case about "somebody" happened in Brussels, and involved the General Manager of a major business unit of a huge European retail marketing operation. He and his 13 year old daughter were walking together one Sunday, talking about the future. He asked his daughter "What kind of family do you want?" At the time, he was thinking to himself "What will I be like as a grandfather?" His daughter stunned him when she said "I'm not going to have any children, because you people have messed the place up, and I'm not going to bring kids into this environment!" That really got his attention. In his case, "somebody" woke up, and he is now managing his business in entirely different ways. It's inside us — "somebody" lives in each of our hearts, and that's where we have to focus the wake up call!

Another very illustrative "somebody" woke up a few years ago in the heart of a Swedish cancer doctor named Karl-Henrik Robèrt. His work is presented in Chapter 4. Dr. Robèrt realized that the cell is the unit which is common to all life on Earth, and that these cells are highly susceptible to chemical toxins and ultraviolet radiation. When he looked into what the environmentalists were saying, he found that for the most part they were debating with each other and were very often in adversarial stances towards business. He likened their approaches to "monkey chatter" among the dying leaves. He pointed out that the withering leaves of the tree were not the problem, but merely a symptom of what was happening in the roots of the tree — the source of the real problem.

With the awakening of his own "somebody," Dr. Robèrt wrote an essay about the natural ecological system that supports all life, that was based on two undisputed scientific laws: the Second Law of Thermodynamics ("stuff" spreads out); and the Law of Conservation of Matter and Energy ("stuff" doesn't go away). That is, the side effects of manufacturing processes are released into the environment as invisible and visible "junk," which the natural system cannot easily reassimilate, so it accumulates.

He sent his essay to a large network of scientists and asked them to tell him what was wrong with his ideas (Dr. Robèrt points out in his presentations that even your worst enemies will give you helpful advice if you ask for it!), which they were happy to do. He did this a

total of 21 times, at which point the readers could offer no more suggestions. He then took this consensus document to the entire population of Sweden, in the form of a brochure, to every household. The
King of Sweden had become so impressed that he financed the production and the mailing. The cyclical processes of manufacturing and
materials handling have today been adopted by many of Sweden's
largest industries and by over 40 Swedish cities! The outputs of the
nonprofit foundation he created, The Natural Step, are also now
taught throughout the Swedish educational system. Dr. Karl-Henrik
Robèrt is an outstanding example of what "somebody" can do, once
awakened.

In order to look further into the awakening of "somebody," I want to
address **mindset as an addiction**. If we're going to get to "somebody,"
we'll each have to deal with the addiction to how we currently think.
We know very well what addiction is — it's a denial, an inner emptiness, a need that never quite gets filled by whatever we're doing to try
to fill it. And it's **all** of us, we're all "addicted" to our mindsets. When
somebody asks us to look at our addictions, we most often say "Stop
nagging me!" or "Mind your own business!" We first have to discover
inside ourselves that we want to do something about those addictions.
When we do find our inner commitment, our inner passion for doing
something, then we become able to take charge of those addictions,
and consciously to make different choices.

Today, at least in the West, we often go to the doctor with chest pains
and say "Fix my chest pains, but don't make me give up all that good
fatty food, don't make me start exercising, don't make me quit smok-
ing, but just take away the pain." Relative to the environment, we say
the same sort of thing — "Somebody ought to fix it, but don't make me
change any of my own habits, don't ask me to consume less."

As one final example, I want to describe the insight garnered by a
friend and colleague regarding how intricately involved we all are,
largely unconsciously, in reinforcing the status quo. My friend arrived
quite late to a meeting in which he was expected to play a key role.

When he eventually arrived, he apologized by saying "I'm sorry to be late, I was being held up by a lot of traffic. If all those cars and trucks hadn't slowed me down, I'd have been here on time!" It took the group several seconds to see the humor in the statement. The other vehicles had slowed him down, and therefore he was also in a vehicle slowing down the others!

First, we have to become aware what our default mindset is, and then we can think about changing it. The challenge in awakening "somebody" is to identify what it would take to think and respond automatically in new, more desirable ways — a task we'll be undertaking in the Chapter 10, where we'll describe the apparent emergence of a whole new outlook that is growing rapidly around the world, and which is predisposed to helping us all to look at the effects of our slumbering "somebodies."

I want to close this chapter with a somewhat poetic statement, the origin of which I do not know, which captures the feeling I want to express in this chapter.

EVERYBODY, SOMEBODY, NOBODY AND ANYBODY

Once upon a time, there were four people.

Their names were:

Everybody

Somebody

Nobody

and Anybody

Whenever there was an important job to be done, Everybody was sure that Somebody would do it. Anybody could have done it, but in the end Nobody did it.

When Nobody did it, Everybody got angry because it was Somebody's job. Everybody thought that Somebody would do it, but Nobody realized that Nobody would do it.

So consequently, Everybody blamed Somebody when Nobody did what Anybody could have done in the first place.

Questions For Contemplation And Dialogue

✦ How can I resist complacency?

✦ Do I have the courage to let go of some of my present "realities" and move into unknown territories?

✦ How do I help people become more aware of their ability to be aware?

✦ Why is it so easy to forget the rapidly growing challenges as I go about my everyday life?

✦ Are my daily activities building sustainability; irrelevant to the future; or destructive of the future?

✦ Am I willing to take personal responsibility for necessary changes?

✦ How *do* I take personal responsibility for the future?

✦ Where can I focus my individual efforts to make the biggest contribution?

✦ How do we awaken a billion somebodies?

✦ What are the gaps between what we say will be necessary and what we are actually doing?

✦ How do we identify and support those who will lead in needed new directions?

✦ What is the role of those in my line of work as the new paradigm emerges?

✦ If people in my line of work were working from a basis of global consciousness, what would we be doing?

✦ What do we want to be able to say about our work 30 years from now?

✦ What am I doing today that will make a positive contribution three years from now?

✦ Will my children be proud of how I spent my career?

✦ What can we do to get the children's voices heard in more arenas?

✧ How can we involve the "owners" of the future — the children — in the creation of the future?

✧ How can we help things fall apart faster so that the re-emergence can happen sooner?

EIGHT

If We Had A Mind To . . .

~

"If we continue to believe as we have always believed, we will continue to act as we have always acted. If we continue to act as we have always acted, we will continue to get what we have always gotten."

MARILYN FERGUSON

"The sustainable state would make fewer demands on our environmental resources, but much greater demands on our moral resources."

HERMAN DALY

Ultimately, the only one we truly can take responsibility for is ourselves. To do this fully in a rapidly changing and unpredictable world, we must develop a facility to make frequent and rapid choices about *how* to think about, and *how* to respond to, the situations we encounter each day. Our mind*sets* have a way of protecting themselves from change, and usually operate like an "autopilot." As far as we know today, we are the only species on Earth which has the capacity to think about *how* we think. Most of the time, however, we don't really engage this capacity; we tend to reinforce our outlooks on life by, for the most part, repeating the same thoughts day after day. In order to take responsibility, then, we must move "from autopilot to choice."

It is clear to a rapidly growing number of people that we can now create virtually *any* reality or future we can envision. It is also becoming clear that we may end life on Earth, as we know it at least, either gradually or cataclysmically. We humans have created a technological capability of amazing power. On the one hand, we can travel to the moon, transplant organs to save lives, and communicate instantly with virtually any part of the planet. On the other hand, we are rapidly degrading our air and water quality, apparently changing the climate on Earth, and damaging our upper atmosphere. We most likely have only a matter of years, rather than generations, to address these challenges.

Technology has helped to increase life expectancy and to reduce dramatically infant and childhood mortality, and thereby contributed to global population growth. In countries where the growth rate is the highest, pressure on the environment for expansion and "Western style" development has led to the understandable and yet massive burning of the rain forests.

Questionable agricultural and food processing methods are increasingly being used to support the demands for more food. And of course we in the West continue to gobble up far more than "our share" of Earth's resources.

Many organizations have formed during the last quarter of the 20th Century which have done a good job of raising the awareness of governments and the public about both the benefits and the challenges we are facing. Even so, most of us don't give the growing challenges much thought on a day to day basis, and those who are aware generally don't feel empowered to act in ways to confront these situations in any serious way in their daily lives. We have done a reasonably good job of preparing for the future technologically. We still have a long way to go psychologically.

In the workplace, we often find that even when strategic plans are created, they are seldom adhered to. We are constantly faced with examples of low integrity and questionable ethics in the arenas of business, finance, government, and even child care. When it comes to the environment, relatively few organizations *voluntarily* restrict themselves in toxic emissions and solid waste disposal; and where regulations exist, minimum compliance (or finding loopholes) unfortunately prevails.

At the personal level, relatively few people on the Earth feel that they are personally responsible for their lot in life. Taking personal initiative for other than personal economic gain, while increasing, is still not widespread. Not enough of us recognize how small and endangered the Earth has become, and even fewer of us realize that there are things we can do locally to alleviate, even in a small way, some of the larger challenges.

In my years of working with individuals in the area of stress management and health promotion, I have often been frustrated with the challenges of influencing individuals to act on the knowledge they already have (e.g. to get plenty of exercise and to avoid tobacco). I have learned that to shift from the status quo, an individual must first "reprogram" her or his mindset so that it supports the habit changes the individual wishes to make.

This chapter asks the question "Why do these situations exist?" Are people by nature self-destructive? Do people generally not care if we degrade the environment until vast tracts become uninhabitable? Are people unconcerned about the legacy we appear to be leaving for our grandchildren? Do people really think that their life style habits won't lead to any consequences? For most people the answer is "No!" to each of these queries, and yet the situation continues to worsen. I believe that the reason for this contradiction lies in our fundamental processes of thinking — our states of consciousness — which we all learn early in our lives. Due to continual, totally normal repetitions and reinforcements, each of us gradually develops a mindset which is persistent and which operates, for the most part, subconsciously.

Whatever mindset we develop influences us to act in ways that are reinforcing of its basic assumptions and values. In other words, *the self-fulfilling prophecy is always at work*, and the longer it works the more absolute our belief systems tend to become. Since this process occurs outside of our awareness most of the time, I like to call it "The Autopilot" mindset.

Computer software is always supplied with certain embedded commands that are called "default settings." Most word processing programs, for example, automatically set the margins on the page at one inch. If a person at the keyboard wishes to change one of these default settings, to create, for example, a two-inch top margin, it must be done intentionally. We can also say that an adult individual's autopilot mindset has a great many default settings, and as with the computer, if we wish to change them we must do so consciously. This book is based on the contention that we must learn to reset several of these default settings, consciously, in order to appreciate more fully the global challenges and to take into account more accurately how our day to day — or even minute to minute — activities are contributing to those challenges.

With conscious choice, one's mindset can become more versatile (that is, appropriately flexible). **Versatility in consciousness** is a key ingredient which needs to be introduced into the educational process at all levels if we are to address the rising worldwide challenges effectively. I want to propose that versatility in consciousness is essential for on-going rapid individual learning and that the only sustainable consciousness is a learning consciousness.

In the following paragraphs, the nature of the autopilot is explored in more detail. Then, six key dimensions of consciousness are introduced; and the value, the liability of over usage, and typical sustaining messages for the extreme poles of each dimension are presented. Also, a series of questions are posed which, when asked repeatedly, can help one move from autopilot to choice — that is, from a fixed, usually non-conscious way of responding to a more conscious and

more versatile way of responding. A systematic process of asking ourselves questions is suggested as an excellent way to "reprogram" our
mindsets so that we learn to operate naturally with more versatility. It
is important to note that the idea is not to reject one way of thinking
for another, but rather to broaden the range of normal thinking available to each of us.

The Nature of The Human Autopilot

A person's autopilot mindset consists of predictable and most often
nonconscious patterns and sequences of thoughts and actions which
are built up over a lifetime, but most rapidly during the first ten or
twelve years of life, through the repetitions of thematic messages and
experiences. My autopilot mindset influences what I perceive, what I
value, and how I process my experiences.

The autopilot, in other words, influences how we experience life in
ways that are *self-fulfilling* and *self-reinforcing*. While a Wall Street bro-
ker and a rural Hindu in Southern India are likely to develop very different mindsets, each one's autopilot is internally consistent and
appropriate to the settings they find themselves in. In each case, their
mindsets operate in ways *that maintain status quo* in their default settings. And in each case, it is quite normal for them to operate, probably without a great deal of awareness, in ways that will *seek to influence
others to see the world the same way they see it.*

This last characteristic of the autopilot can cause a lot of conflict,
because whenever it is operating, we are likely to make views different
from our own "wrong" and perhaps act to "set the other person right,"
usually to no avail! These senseless conflicts are among the major contributors to unnecessary stress in relationships.

While each person's autopilot mindset is a perfectly normal reflection of his or her life experiences, and may work just fine when no
changes are called for, it is often necessary to increase versatility and
choose different ways of perceiving and processing experiences when
the external world demands changes. Routine daily activities are

made much easier and more efficient by the functioning of the human autopilot. For example, driving a car, after several years' experience, is much easier than it was the first few times behind the wheel. But when new actions are called for or novel situations must be addressed (e.g. driving for the first time in a country that uses the opposite of the road), the autopilot default settings usually do not provide the most effective state of consciousness.

Any "reprogramming" of the autopilot will require the same processes that established it in the first place — repetitions of messages and experiences. Since it is normal for the human mindset autopilot to attempt to maintain itself, it will be necessary that the repetitions of the new ideas and intentions be carried out consciously. Often, it is very useful to create structures or disciplines that require that the new repetitions are carried out in order to get beyond the status quo maintenance efforts of the old autopilot. One example would be to identify a habit pattern that isn't yielding the results you want (the default setting). Then describe a new personal "policy" you wish to replace the old habit with. And then require yourself to spend, as an example, thirty minutes every Tuesday at 9:00 p.m. contemplating the eventual consequences of the newly adopted policy. After several weeks of doing this, it will become a natural part of your mindset. Without this amount of discipline, it is likely that your intended new habit will soon be forgotten.

It is probably easiest to change one default message at a time. Wholesale changes of one's consciousness, that is, a complete personal transformation, is possible and sometimes happens, but step by step change is probably going to be a lot easier to assimilate for most of us.

Some Key Dimensions of Consciousness

In the following paragraphs, six key dimensions of human consciousness are described which reflect the themes that have emerged as I have asked a large number of groups to brainstorm the prevailing default mindsets which they experience most often around them.

They also reflect the mindsets which most naturally create and reinforce the present realities we have explored in the early chapters of this book. There are certainly additional dimensions that could be included, but these six seem to cover almost all of the defaults that arise in these brainstorming sessions.

As mentioned in the Foreword, the brainstormed list of default settings usually is dominated by items like short term, superficial, greedy, impatient, and cynical. When I then ask the brainstorming groups what life would be like twenty or thirty years into the future if these default settings were to continue, the group members always paint a pretty grim picture of what everyday life will be like. But if we consider items like those brainstormed to be the left ends of a series of dimensions, an understanding is created which allows for choosing how to repond from along a continuum of possibilities. For example, one possible dimension could be:

CYNICAL _____**TOLERANT**

With this viewpoint, we can ask ourselves "What is my 'zone of comfort' (level of versatility) along each of these dimensions?" and "How could I widen my present zone of comfort?"

I want to point out that these prevailing autopilot positions are perfectly normal and understandable. They are products of the prevailing mode of Western thought that has developed over the last 400 or so years since Copernicus and others began the process of shifting our understanding that the Earth is not the center of the universe. Descartes and Newton subsequently set off a movement to understand everything in the universe except the human spirit (which was left to the church) in machine-mathematical models.

When the external situation is relatively stable, which was the prevailing state in human history until quite recently, and there are relatively few internal pressures for change, the autopilot positions operate reasonably successfully. However, when turbulence is introduced, the status quo maintaining qualities of the collective autopilot work against effectiveness, and even against survival.

On each of the following six dimensions, our educations and on-going socialization processes tend to reinforce default "zones of comfort" towards the extreme **LEFT** sides of the continuum. Once again, it is proposed that the kind of consciousness which fosters on-going learning and enquiry, *a sustainable consciousness*, is one which operates with a wide zone of comfort. For example, "Versatility" means being able to hold both a cynical and a tolerant viewpoint at the same time, and from this range, making a conscious response.

Pressure and stress often compress or narrow one's zones of comfort and push them to one extreme or the other on a given dimension. For example, someone who seems always to be in a hurry may become panic stricken and overwhelmed by mounting deadlines and an "absence of enough time." Someone who is mildly prejudiced against certain groups may become more closed minded and more radically hateful. Conversely, enquiry and involvement often facilitate a broadening of one's zone of comfort, by providing new insights and unexpected vantage points.

1. TIME ORIENTATION

SHORT TERM _____ LONG TERM

The **Short Term** end of this continuum suggests a focus on immediate deadlines, immediate priorities, and a sense of urgency. Difficulties and deviations from desired results are dealt with in an expedient, "quick fix" manner. There is a great deal of emphasis placed on efficiency now, with little or no thought given to future consequences. The 10:00 meeting always takes precedence over the longer range considerations. Since speed of response is paramount in this mindset, the quick fixes tend to provide only temporary symptomatic relief, as the deliberateness needed to get below the surface of a situation is viewed as taking too much time.

> MESSAGES THAT CREATE/MAINTAIN: Don't fix it if it ain't broke. Just do it.

QUESTIONS TO HELP FOCUS: What needs attention now? What are your immediate priorities?

VALUE: Establishing priorities. Acting with efficiency.

RESULT OF OVERUSE: Lose the big picture. Overlook long term consequences. Put bandages on symptoms.

The **Long Term** end of this continuum suggests a focus on long term consequences and establishing long term goals and directions for the future. Difficulties and deviations are placed in the context of the long range view. Behaviors which contribute to the realization of a vision are encouraged, as are those which explore contingencies and possibilities. The role of a "leader" is most often involved with changing the established order of something. To do this in any purposeful way requires a future orientation with a strong sense of purpose and direction.

MESSAGES WHICH CREATE/MAINTAIN: Be prepared. Plan ahead.

QUESTIONS WHICH HELP FOCUS: What do you anticipate? Where are we headed? Where do we want to go?

VALUE: Anticipation, prediction, possibilities, contingencies.

RESULT OF OVERUSE: Lose timely responsiveness. Ignore pressing realities.

2. RESPONSIVENESS

REACTIVE _____ CREATIVE

When a person is focused on the **Reactive** end of this dimension, he or she is primarily focused on external stimuli, either adhering to or rebelling against the prevailing rules and structures. This response emphasizes consistency, and reacts promptly to events as they happen to correct deviations. A person operating reactively is motivated by external concerns and/or by existing nonconscious patterns or "scripts." This mindset generally desires predictability and consistency, and prefers "tried and true" approaches to situations.

> MESSAGES WHICH CREATE/MAINTAIN: Do as you're told. If it feels good, do it. Life's a bitch and then you die.
>
> QUESTIONS TO HELP FOCUS: What is the established policy, procedure, or practice? What has been done before in this kind of situation?
>
> VALUE: Consistency, responsiveness, loyalty.
>
> RESULT OF OVERUSE: Stuck in a rut. Unable to flow with change.

When a person focuses on the **Creative** end of this dimension, he or she is primarily focused on taking initiatives and will choose to be guided by his or her own inner ideas of how to proceed. This mindset emphasizes the articulation of desired outcomes and spends a great deal of time in innovation and in envisioning possibilities. When operating from this mindset, one responds to situations by reflecting on the larger picture and making up an appropriate response. This mindset also calls for a great deal of challenge and novelty in everyday life, and there is often a dislike of using the same procedure or methods repeatedly.

> MESSAGES WHICH CREATE/MAINTAIN: Be your own person. You can be anything you want to be.
>
> QUESTIONS TO HELP FOCUS: Is there a different or better approach? What would you do about this situation if you had a magic wand?
>
> VALUE: Innovation, new ideas, new directions.
>
> RESULT OF OVERUSE: Overlook proven processes. Reinvent the wheel.

3. FOCUS OF ATTENTION

LOCAL _____ GLOBAL

The **Local** end of this continuum suggests thinking that is narrow and parochial. Attention to situations is framed in egoistic terms such as "What's in it for me (or us)?" There is a sense of exclusiveness, and most situations include an "US" and a "THEM." Like attracts like, and groups form around similarities. Boundaries are drawn around differences. Thus, looking out for number one, our team or department, or our company, are of paramount importance. I once met a manager who told me that her department was always so busy fighting with another department down the hall that they all had lost sight of the "real threat" coming from the competing organization down the street!

> MESSAGES WHICH CREATE/MAINTAIN: Look out for number one. You've got to expect that from a _____!
>
> QUESTIONS TO HELP FOCUS: What makes you different or unique? What is your special contribution?
>
> VALUE: Survival, protection, maintaining position.
>
> RESULT OF OVERUSE: Loss of perspective, ethnocentrism, exclusion of potential resources.

The **Global** end of this continuum suggests thinking that is broad and ecumenical. Attention to situations is framed holistically, as being embedded in a larger context. There is a sense of inclusiveness, and a broad array of people and factors are included in reaching decisions. Heterogeneity and diversity are highly valued.

In this mindset, one is aware that eating a typical fast food meal may be contributing to the release of ozone gobbling CFCs from the styrofoam packaging; that the rain forests are being burned, adding to global warming, to provide more space for growing cattle to feed the Northern hemisphere's seemingly insatiable desire for beef; that burning these forests destroys migratory bird habitats, thus diminishing flocks and thereby increasing the number of insects and the use of insecticides; and that over half the fresh water consumed in the U.S. is used directly or indirectly by the livestock industry. The global perspective never loses sight of the possible far-reaching effects of "local" actions, and reminds us that on planet Earth there isn't any "there" anymore — that everything is connected to everything else.

> MESSAGES WHICH CREATE/MAINTAIN: Don't miss the forest for the trees. Let's keep things in perspective.

> QUESTIONS TO HELP FOCUS: Can you describe the big picture? How can you make a difference in the world?

> VALUE: Comprehensive view, inclusiveness.

> RESULT OF OVERUSE: Idealism. Loss of initiative or drive. Inattention to detail.

4. PREVAILING LOGIC

SEPARATION _____ SYSTEMIC

The **Separation,** or **Either/Or,** end of this dimension suggests ever increasing specialization and thinking is predominantly in the rational/analytic mode. Situations are broken down into their smallest parts as a means to understanding the whole, and difficulties are addressed "locally" without consideration of influences that are more distant in time or space. This approach to logic grew out of the Cartesian-Newtonian tradition, which at its peak spawned "the scientific method," and is based on using logic and focusing on observable (tangible) facts. The effects of this mindset on professions and work roles has been the proliferation of ever increasing specialization, with each focusing on ever more precise spheres of attention.

> MESSAGES WHICH CREATE/MAINTAIN: The best way to understand something is to take it apart. A place for everything, and everything in its place.

> QUESTIONS TO HELP FOCUS: What are the relevant facts in

this situation? What do you get when you "crunch the numbers?"

VALUE: Convergence, specialization, rationality.

RESULT OF OVERUSE: Fragmentation, low synergy, get lost in minutiae.

The **Systemic,** or **Both/And,** end of this dimension suggests ever increasing generalization, and thinking is focused on understanding how the interaction of the parts contributes to the operating results of the whole. Situations are viewed as being complex, having both internal dynamics and interactions with their external environments. Broad cause and effect relationships are sought out, which may have no common sense or bearing on the symptoms at hand. This approach to logic is growing out of the realization that reductionist thinking often misses the root causes in complex situations, and ends up generating a never ending supply of symptoms (or "brush fires"). The systemic mindset works towards completing the bigger picture, and is based on the holistic idea that everything is ultimately connected to everything else.

MESSAGES WHICH CREATE/MAINTAIN: Solving one problem almost always creates others. "The shin bone's connected to the knee bone..."

QUESTIONS TO HELP FOCUS: Who are the key stakeholders? If we take this action, what consequences can we predict?

VALUE: Divergent, holistic, finding interrelationships and interdependencies.

RESULT OF OVERUSE: Equate models to reality. Get lost in the clouds of complexity.

5. ERROR RESPONSE

JUSTIFICATION _____ **ACKNOWLEDGMENT**

At the **Justification** end of this dimension, one expresses the need for self-protection, and operates in ways to convince others that one is not to blame when errors become evident. Actions are taken to shift the responsibility to other parties or to circumstances which are beyond one's control. In corporations, large legal fees are often expended to fight government directives, such as to reduce environmental pollution, rather than spending to implement the directive.

This mindset reflects a need to find out who is wrong or to blame whenever something goes wrong. When one who is operating in this mindset makes a mistake or is accused of wrongdoing, the first response is to justify why the action was actually "OK."

> MESSAGES WHICH CREATE/MAINTAIN: It's not my fault! All right, who's to blame here?

> QUESTIONS TO HELP FOCUS: What are your reasons for your actions? What's wrong with this picture?

> VALUE: Judgement, law, and rule enforcement.

> RESULT OF OVERUSE: Win/Lose polarization. Risk aversion.

At the **Acknowledgment** end of this dimension, one expresses the need for learning and operates in ways to ensure learning. When others make mistakes, forgiveness is readily forthcoming, with the emphasis being placed on learning and moving on. After making a mistake, someone who is operating from this mindset will admit to it, reflect on the consequences, and look for ways to get back on track. In this mindset, one's inner dialogue is affirming and developmental. The overall orientation is one of unconditional acceptance of self and others, and emphasis is placed on healing and on building strength.

> MESSAGES WHICH CREATE/MAINTAIN: To err is human, to forgive divine. Let one who is without sin cast the first stone.

> QUESTIONS TO HELP FOCUS: What can you learn from this experience? How might you benefit from letting go of that grudge?

> VALUE: Ease of exploration, love, growth, learning.

RESULT OF OVERUSE: Easily taken advantage of. Self sacrificing. Loss of discipline.

6. LIFE ORIENTATION

DOING/HAVING _____ BEING

On the **Doing/Having** side of this continuum, the quest in life is to acquire tangible goods as the primary vehicle to realizing satisfaction and fulfillment. Activity is valued and is rewarded by the ability to acquire material possessions. Of course, from this perspective, one *never* has enough material possessions. Articles are considered in terms of who "owns" them, and success in life is defined in terms of "winning" and being financially comfortable. This mindset is driven by the technological imperative which suggests that if we can do something technologically, we should go ahead and do it — and if troubles arise, we'll be able to solve them with further technology. The extreme of this mindset is captured by the bumper sticker which reads "The one who dies with the most toys wins."

> MESSAGES WHICH CREATE/MAINTAIN: What's in it for me? Faster, cheaper, better!

> QUESTIONS TO HELP FOCUS: What is the most cost-effective thing to do? What's the bottom line?

> VALUE: Financial performance and material comforts.

> RESULT OF OVERUSE: Attachment. Possessiveness. Loss of human sensitivity. Burnout.

On the **Being** end of this continuum, the quest in life is for the acquisition of insight — perspective and understanding of what life is all about spiritually. Material items, such as homes, cars, and the Earth, are considered in terms of custodianship — "It's in my possession for the time being, and it's up to me to maintain or improve it while I am its custodian." Success in life, from this perspective, comes from self-realization. This mindset first considers how a given decision contributes to the "greater good" and expresses a desire for harmony among people and with the Earth. Being of service to others is given priority, and life in all its forms is held to be sacred.

> MESSAGES WHICH CREATE/MAINTAIN: You'll never walk alone. Trust the process. As ye sow, so shall ye reap.

> QUESTIONS TO HELP FOCUS: What really matters in your life? What does your "higher self" say about this?

> VALUE: Self realization, transcendent viewpoint.

> RESULT OF OVERUSE: Become ungrounded. Lose touch with "mainstream."

As already mentioned, due to our education and upbringing, most of us find that our default "settings" are more towards the left ends of these dimensions, and that our "zones of comfort" are rather narrow. There is obviously no single position on any of these dimensions which is always going to be the best or most effective position. The challenge that we each face is to become more aware of the consequences of nearly always behaving unconsciously from our default settings. When most of us read a book on goal setting or participate in a seminar on systems thinking, or attend a lecture on water quality, we immediately think "Gee, that's really important!" But within a few hours, if we are still thinking about these ideas, most of us are likely to be thinking "Somebody ought to do something about that," as our temporarily expanded awareness snaps back to its default settings — the autopilot mindset.

As we develop a greater awareness of just what our default positions are, we make available to ourselves more choices about **HOW** to think. The issue is not in having or not having the "correct" default settings, but in having awareness of them and being able to choose other ways of responding that may be more appropriate to the situation. Each end of these dimensions has some pluses and some liabilities, as outlined above.

One of the best ways to promote increased versatility or expanded zones of comfort in our mindsets is to ask ourselves questions regularly which will take our mindsets to more distant parts of each continuum. I would propose that questions such as those suggested above, in relation to each dimension, be embedded in our educational processes from the very earliest years. The questions for contemplation and dialogue which follow, also promote versatility of thinking and a broader sense of self awareness.

Courses in increasing mindset versatility could be built around questions such as these. They can also be included in virtually any adult education or worksite training program and, when present, will most likely enhance the effectiveness of the course material as well as promoting mindset versatility.

In summary, we have the means to create just about any future we desire. We also have the means to bring an end to life on Earth. We know basically what comprises the interacting web of global challenges, and we have the means to deal systemically with them. *The primary reason that we are neither creating our ideal future nor effectively addressing the challenges facing us has to do with the nature of human consciousness.*

As we grow up and develop our values, beliefs, expectations, and assumptions about life, we develop a consistent outlook, or mindset. Over the years, this mindset receives so much reinforcement that it becomes second nature and operates without our paying much attention to it. It becomes an autopilot guiding our experiences, perceptions, and behaviors. The autopilot mindset operates in a self-protective way, seeking to maintain itself and to convince others that they should hold the same mindset.

Due to our education and upbringing, the prevailing autopilot mindset is most often focused on the material, the local, and the short term. It is further most often focused on reacting to external circumstances, on logical analysis, and on justifying our mistakes and seeking to shift responsibility to others. These default outlooks may be relatively effective when everything is going along smoothly, when there are no complex challenges or obstacles, and when no changes are called for. When complexity creates a rough road, when there are lots of hassles, and when changes are needed, this autopilot mindset is most likely to "dig in" and protect itself, perhaps going so far as to agree that "Somebody ought to do something about that..."

In order to address the situation that is emerging today, more mindset versatility is becoming essential. A good way to promote this versatility is to get into the habit of regularly asking ourselves and each other questions which take our consciousness out of autopilot and into choice before deciding how to proceed.

Questions For Contemplation And Dialogue

✧ How much am I *willing* to change my lifestyle today? How much will I *have* to change my lifestyle tomorrow?

✧ What are my most important values and how well expressed are they in my chosen work?

✧ Am I aware of and true to my own values? Do we model what we "preach" — do we walk our values' talk?

✧ How shall we maintain optimism and hope in the face of growing challenges?

✧ What is the true meaning of Life? Consciousness?

✧ How do I stay connected to my passion in order to stick with the changes I need to make?

✧ How can we draw on our innate spirituality, i.e. something larger than ourselves, to become more consistently proactive?

✧ Do I have the courage to let go of a mindset that has been "good" to me?

✧ What am I willing to change within myself in order to help the dreams of our children become a reality?

✧ What are my addictions? Am I willing to let them go?

✧ How can I look at the "emptiness" within that I sometimes feel?

✧ What risks am I willing to take to raise "uncomfortable" questions about our widespread addiction to endless growth?

✧ To what lengths will I go to break my denial and recover from my addictions?

✧ How can we mobilize the healing of the individual so that the collective can begin to heal?

✧ Can we apply the AA principles of group support to deliver the message and encourage consciousness change?

✧ What is the role of the "heart" in sustainable consciousness?

✧ How can we foster a widely shared mindset that cares for/about all?

✧ How can we begin to accurately assess the mindset defaults that are actually in operation?

✧ What do we already know about how to facilitate the emergence of new mindsets?

✧ What practices can I adopt to promote versatility of mindset?

✧ What can we do to facilitate receiving the necessary disconfirmations?

✧ What is our role, if any, in helping others to establish their own sustainable consciousness?

✧ What are we doing that perpetuates the short term, selfish mindset?

✧ How do we help people adopt longer time frames?

✧ How shall I stop the habit of acquiring when appearances/things are the artifacts of our culture?

✧ Do I really need to have this new/bigger/faster/more expensive thing?

✧ How shall we interconnect personal needs with global needs to foster a new mindset?

✧ How shall we help men and women balance their masculine and feminine energies and find harmony with each other?

✧ How shall we shift mindsets from "doing/having" to a more "being/relationship focus?

✧ What can I do to reshape my attitudes about other living species?

✧ We need to be regularly asking ourselves and each other "What's really important?"

✧ Ask more How?/Why?/Who? questions and fewer What?/When? questions!

✧ How can we sustain versatility of consciousness, especially in times of plenty?

✧ Is my line of work an "enabler" of a dysfunctional process?

SECTION IV

Thinking Into The Future

IN MOST WORKPLACES TODAY, THE THINGS THAT ARE REWARDED INCLUDE short-term focus, fast cycle time, efficiency and speed, shareholder return, a narrow/local perspective, and cost containment and reduction by the most expedient means available. These "default settings" in the corporate culture go a long way towards determining what portion of an employee's total being is sought after and reinforced. The human resources of the organization are seen in many places as replacement parts rather than as whole beings.

Those aspects of human functioning and being that would more effectively facilitate sustainable high level performance during turbulent times are generally not recognized as being important: meaningful work, human dignity and integrity, tracking the invisible costs of human depletion, long term awareness (10-20 year focus), and true systems or big picture thinking. As a result, organizations today may be expected to focus their energies on immediate needs for survival at the expense of longer-term survival prospects. **Trying harder and harder to get positive results, using approaches that are working less and less effectively, eventually leads to diminishing returns.**

How will the historians regard our era at the turn the century? As a passing storm leading to a bright new day? As a period of turbulence preceding steady decline into chaos and despair? The opportunities are unparalleled in human history — but there is no guarantee of a golden age of prosperity, as the "Post Moderns" may shake our culture to pieces. The challenges, too, are unparalleled in human history — but sliding into a morass is not inevitable — as a growing portion of our population is poised (although "it" doesn't realize this yet) to trigger a renaissance.

One thing we cannot have much longer is "more of the same," as few of the present trends outlined in this book are sustainable for much longer.

The qualities of our dominant images of the future, and the qualities of the efforts based on them; will create whatever future we do have. As we know very well, our outlooks and worldviews tend to be self-fulfilling, and a lot depends on how optimistic or pessimistic our predominant future view is. In *The Image of the Future*, Fred Polak (1973) found that pessimistic societies, historically, have deteriorated rather quickly, and that basically optimistic societies have been able to thrive.

This closing section of the book takes a last look at the effect of today's prevailing expectations about work and the worker in Chapter 9, detailing some of the adverse consequences that are occurring with increasing frequency. It concludes in Chapter 10 with a hopeful look at the emergence of a whole new consciousness that will be better equipped to take on the challenges of the 21st Century.

Questions For Contemplation And Dialogue

- ✧ Why do we focus on our own selfish habits rather than on the needs of the next generation?
- ✧ What new tools will we need in my line of work to have a useful role in the future?
- ✧ How and with whom can I develop collaborative relationships that support balance and sustainable consciousness?
- ✧ How do we need to redefine our line of work beyond the single organization framework to the global context as the true customer or client?

✧ How often have we pushed our organizations to become more "green?"

✧ How can we provide meaningful involvement in society for those without work?

✧ In what ways is my present life style symptomatic of the essential challenges?

✧ In what ways is our organization's work process symptomatic of the essential challenges?

NINE

The Hurrier I Go
The Behinder I Get

"It is our job to make women feel unhappy with what they have — everything from their eyelashes, to their nose pores, to their weight, to last season's clothes. . ."

ADVERTISING EXECUTIVE

British ecologist Edward Goldsmith (1993) points out that every biological system develops a "critical path" it must follow to experience optimal conditions. Significant deviations from this path cause seemingly intractable problems for that biological system. There is growing awareness today that the entire planet Earth, as a biological system, has been taken off of its critical path by human activity, and that the complex and seemingly unresolvable challenges arising in our environmental and economic systems are *symptomatic* of this. At the level of the enterprise, the most obvious current manifestation of this deviation from the critical path is the ever-increasing demand on almost every employed person to *do more, more quickly, and with fewer resources.* These heightened pressures on us as individuals are *not* resolving the challenges, but they *are* resulting in widespread trauma at work, and a population, at least in the U.S., that is cranky much of the time.

In the vast majority of cases, when someone is hired, the organization really only wants to rent a small portion of that person's "being" for a certain number of hours per day. Over the years, much attention has been given to creating structures and designing relationships among people at work that will allow for the efficient creation of products or services. This requires that people at work behave in predictable ways, with as much of their behavior as possible being devoted to getting some specified slice of the work done.

Position descriptions are generally very specific, and usually do not call for creativity, adaptability, emotionality, intuition, or expressions of the human spirit. In other words, only a little portion of each of us is being rented. We are expected to bring our bodies and our logical minds into work, and to leave the rest of ourselves in our cars! Usually, when things are going well, these rented portions of our being are able to perform pretty effectively. However, when the environment is unpredictable, due to economic, environmental, social or political turbulence, the rented parts may not include those aspects of one's being that are necessary for the most effective coping.

As was pointed out in the introduction to this section, in most workplaces today, the things that are rewarded include short-term focus, fast cycle time, efficiency and speed, shareholder return, a narrow/local perspective, and cost containment and reduction by the most expedient means available. These "default settings" in the corporate culture go a long way towards determining what portion of an employee's total being is sought after and reinforced. The human resources of the organization are seen in many places merely as replacement parts rather than as whole beings.

Those aspects of human functioning and being that would more effectively facilitate sustainable high level performance during turbulent times generally are not recognized as being important: meaningful work, human dignity and integrity, tracking the invisible costs of human depletion, long term awareness (10-20 year focus), and true systems or big picture thinking. As a result, organizations today may be expected to focus their energies on immediate needs for survival at the expense of longer-term survival prospects. **Trying harder and harder to get positive results, using approaches that are working less and less effectively, eventually leads to diminishing returns.**

As a reflection of this increasingly frustrating process of trying to keep the organization's "head above water," there are more apparent burnouts and pressure related casualties in the workplace today than at any time in recent history. People are being asked to adjust to continuous reorganizations; and "survivors" of "right-sizing" exercises are being asked to accomplish ever more with ever fewer resources. A few years ago, people in organizations were eagerly signing up for stress management courses. Today, however, terms such as "stress" and "burnout" are often taboo. The implied message is frequently that one should be pleased to even have a job, and that the added pressures of the contemporary workplace should be taken on with a "stiff upper lip." Those who have lost their jobs have generally been unable to find new work at the same level of pay and benefits as they had been receiving.

Several years ago I developed and tested a questionnaire, which I called "The Strain Response," that measures the amount of physical depletion an individual is experiencing as a result of the stress in their lives. After collecting thousands of scores in the late 1970s, I established percentiles and compared the health statuses over time of people in different percentile groups (Adams, 1978).

I wanted to find out, for example, if people in the 20th percentile (those whose scores were lower than 80% of the population) experienced better physical health over a period of time than those in the 80th percentile (those whose scores were higher than 80% of the population). After a number of such investigations, I concluded that *people who chronically had scores above the 50th percentile were at significantly greater risk of experiencing adverse health changes than those below the 50th percentile.* Very high scores suggest "withdrawals" are being made from one's health account, and very low scores suggest "deposits" are being placed into the account. I also found that people's strain scores were strongly correlated to their levels of stress. For most people, high levels of stress leads to a high strain score; and high strain, in turn, eventually leads to changes in health.

Some people, however, maintained relatively low strain scores even with high levels of stress. They also seemed to enjoy continued good health regardless of their pressures. It turned out that these people invariably had very healthy lifestyle habits — they ate balanced diets and exercised a lot. They were not overweight, and didn't smoke or drink alcohol. Many of them meditated. These findings added a considerable amount of credibility to my work with measuring people's levels of stress and offering seminars in how to manage stress.

But something happened during the late 80's and early 90's that was puzzling to a number of people who were using the strain questionnaire in their corporate seminars. As time passed, they found that gradually increasing numbers of their employees, *regardless of their lifestyle habits*, were scoring higher than the 50th percentile on The Strain Response. I began receiving calls informing me that "Something was wrong with my percentiles." Upon reflection, I concluded that the only thing "wrong" with the percentiles was that they had been established in about 1978, when workplace stress was relatively lower. I doubt that people have evolved much physically over these years, so I suggested to my callers that their populations must be experiencing very high levels of stress. They agreed with this, and some also pointed out that there were more frequent illnesses, both minor and major, both episodic and chronic, in their employee groups. The Strain Response questionnaire is included here for interested readers to complete.

The following list of conditions will give you an indication of how much your present experiences of stress are depleting your reserves. Rate yourself from 1 to 5, depending on how frequently each item has been true for you *during the past two or three weeks.*

1 = Rarely or never

2 = Occasionally

3 = Sometimes

4 = Frequently

5 = Nearly always

_____ 1. Eat too much.

_____ 2. Drink to much alcohol (non-alcohol users use 1).

_____ 3. Smoke more than usual (non-smokers use 1).

_____ 4. Feel tense, uptight, fidgety, and nervous.

_____ 5. Feel depressed or remorseful.

_____ 6. Like myself less.

_____ 7. Have difficulty going to sleep or staying asleep.

_____ 8. Feel restless and unable to concentrate.

_____ 9. Have decreased interest in sex.

_____ 10. Have increased interest in sex.

_____ 11. Have loss of appetite.

_____ 12. Feel tired, low energy, excessive fatigue.

_____ 13. Feel irritable.

_____ 14. Think about suicide.

_____ 15. Become less communicative.

_____ 16. Feel disoriented or overwhelmed.

_____ 17. Have difficulty getting up in the morning.

_____ 18. Have headaches.

_____ 19. Have upset stomach or intestinal problems.

_____ 20. Have sweaty and/or trembling hands.

_____ 21. Have shortness of breath or sighing.

_____ 22. Let things slide, procrastinate.

_____ 23. Show misdirected anger.

_____ 24. Feel "unhealthy."

_____ 25. Feel weak.

_____ 26. Feel dizzy or lightheaded.

_____   TOTAL STRAIN SCORE

PERCENTILE	SCORE	
10	33	
20	37	
30	41	
40	45	
50	49	*beginning level of health risk*
60	52	
70	57	
80	62	
90	69	

Each item on the strain response may arise as a result of over taxing the endocrine system, especially the thyroid and adrenal glands, through a prolonged, continuous triggering of the fight or flight response. You may recognize a few of these conditions as being especially true for you from time to time. These are your "red flags." It is useful to become aware of when you get these early warning signals. Their presence indicates that your strain level is getting too high and that you could benefit by getting rid of some avoidable stressors, coping with the unavoidable ones more effectively, and building up your health reserves so that you can better withstand the pressure.

At the time I wrote this book, it was not unusual in my own corporate seminars for all but a few participants to score above that presumed threshold of health risk. Simultaneously, more and more people were reporting to me that they had never felt so stressed out in their lives, and that there was really no one they could turn to at work to talk about what was going on with them. If we rule out the idea that good eating and exercise habits no longer work, we can only conclude that workplace stress has grown to levels beyond the protective capabilities of the obvious lifestyle factors!

Five different types of response are necessary simultaneously, if we are to respond effectively to such pressure packed situations. We must treat the personal symptoms arising from these pressures as we encounter them; and we must learn to operate in ways that build capacity and protect well being over the longer term. In other words, we need to learn how to support individuals at work in today's unpredictable environment, in ways that *also* build their capacities to thrive over the long term. The five essential focuses include: self management, for building and protecting health; novelty management, for living with frequent changes; habit management, for avoiding ruts and altering unuseful patterns; performance management, for achieving and maintaining optimal personal performance; and life management, for ensuring meaning and good quality relationships.

The Immediate Response

It seems that by now most organizations that are interested have already offered health protection and stress management courses to their employees. **In today's environment, when more and more people are saying they are really "stressed out," it usually doesn't occur to them to refresh themselves on the principles that were included, or to bring updated programs back for another round of offerings.** It seems to me that this is just what is needed. In this section I want to review the five essential kinds of responses for "surfing on the waves of change." 1. Self Management, 2. Novelty Management, 3. Habit Management, 4. Performance Management, and 5. Life Management.

1. SELF MANAGEMENT: Stress does not cause health problems or diminish performance — it is the accumulation of tension associated with *unexpressed "fight or flight"* preparation (strain) which eventually wears people down.

One side effect of the prolonged accumulation of strain is that the muscles held in tension around the torso restrict proper breathing. Since the brain uses up over 25% of the oxygen carried by the blood, it begins to suffocate, and sends an appeal for oxygen via an impulse to the diaphragm. This results in a sigh (or sometimes a yawn) which is an almost universal signal of excessive prolonged pressure. Whenever there is sighing, there is loss of performance accuracy. A "**breathing break**" consisting of a brisk walk or a few flights of stairs will help to alleviate the strain.

Prolonged strain is a reflection of an accumulation of "fight or flight" hormones circulating in the system. A regular physical exercise program, which is a socially acceptable form of "flight," actually uses up that accumulation, thereby reducing strain. Walking two or three miles at a brisk pace (or the equivalent) three to five times a week is usually all that is needed.

One of my clients, a plant manager, actually insisted that employees who came to his office in a seemingly stressed state take a brisk five minute walk before he would talk to them. He felt strongly that these walks made a big difference in how much he was able to help these employees.

The stress response is triggered by messages coming from the autonomic nervous system. Regular relaxation practices, such as prayer, meditation, music, reading and so on, can teach one how to reverse the autonomic message, and thereby control the degree of "fight or flight" experienced. Regular practice is necessary, as the internal learning process is both cumulative and quickly lost.

The final basic message of health management has to do with diet. The water-soluble vitamins, the Bs and C, cannot be stored in the body and have to be consumed everyday. Under stress, there is evidence that the body burns up these nutrients at a much faster pace than normal. Further, if one uses alcohol, tobacco, sugar and/or caffeine as "stress crutches," the B and C vitamins are further incapacitated in being able to go about their work in the body (about 50 crucial functions have been identified for each of these vitamins). Most of these nutrients are contained in fruits, vegetables and grains, which currently only comprise about 10-15% of the calories in the average "Western" diet. Nutritionists tell us that at least 60% of our calories should come from these complex carbohydrates.

2. NOVELTY MANAGEMENT: Whenever people are confronted with the necessity for making changes, they are likely to experience at least some degree of what I call "Novelty." I define novelty as the amount of surprise in a change and the amount of uncertainty or unfamiliarity created by the new situation. Changes are stressful to the extent that they create novelty. An expected change which the person has undertaken several times before will create less novelty and hence less stress than a surprise change which leads one into an unknown situation.

To get back on top of life as quickly as possible, it is important to manage the novelty associated with the change. In order to do this, there are four essential questions that must be answered to cope effectively: 1.) What **information** will be required in the new situation and where can I get it? 2.) What new **skills** will be required by the emerging situation and how will I develop them? 3.) What do I need to do to create and maintain a **positive attitude** during the period of adjustment. 4.) What can I do to **flow smoothly with necessary changes**?

I once did a study which indicated that people who had inaccurate expectations about what was going to transpire adjusted **just as well** as those who had accurate expectations, so long as they were also flexible about changing those expectations as new information became available. People who had no expectations at all had the most trouble adjusting. Therefore, keeping people in the dark because "We don't know exactly what will happen" is more likely to contribute to burnout and lowered productivity than is the message:

"Here is our best estimate of how things will develop. We're going to act as if this is accurate, and we're asking you to remain flexible — we'll be letting you know as soon as possible when new information requiring different expectations becomes available."

"Until further notice" information is **far** more effective than no information in helping people to maintain high levels of performance and well-being during times of change.

Many changes also require people to behave differently. They may no longer be called on to use the same talents they were regularly putting to use before the change transpired. Instead, they may be asked to develop and use new skills. For example, when one is given a new job on a new project, one may have to learn a new computer program, or how to work with a more permissive boss. Spending some time during the process of change assessing what skills will be needed in the new setting, and figuring out how to develop them as quickly as possible, can make a huge contribution to reducing novelty.

It may be important for the person adjusting to a change to take a skill-building course, or to ask someone who has already made a similar change to give them some advice on how best to cope with the new situation. In order to fill this need there are today support groups for just about every change imaginable! Changes are taking place so rapidly today that much of what one learns while in school becomes obsolete in just a few years or even months. Some corporations have realized this and created "universities" of their own to help employees keep up with the need to continuously update their knowledge and skills. Of course, it is also up to each of us to create our own "universities" for ourselves.

As I have been suggesting throughout this book, our attitudes or outlooks tend to be self-fulfilling. If we look for problems, we will find them. If we expect to be devastated by a change, we probably will be. On the other hand, if we look for opportunities, we are just as likely to find them. If we expect to learn and grow from a change, and become a more able person as a result of our experiences, then that will be our experience.

Figure 10 may be useful in understanding this. Our beliefs about reality and our expectations strongly influence the ways in which we experience and interpret a given situation. And the ways in which we experience and interpret a situation, in turn, strongly reinforces our beliefs about the nature of reality and our expectations. It is in this way that the autopilot nature of our mental functioning reinforces the present outlook and works against our developing new, more versatile ways to think about the experiences in our lives.

Figure 10 — The Relationshp Among Perceptions, Experiences and Mindset

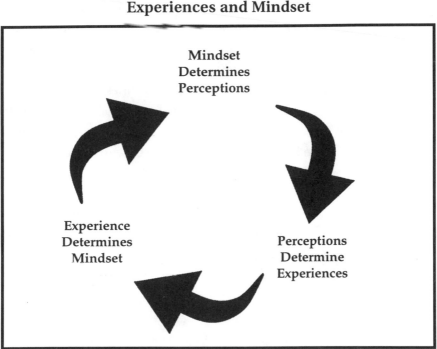

It should therefore be clear that a positive, optimistic, and confident outlook will allow one to handle a high novelty change far more expeditiously than a negative, pessimistic, and powerless outlook. There have been dozens of popular books published over the past twenty years, and thousands of workshops, that have presented a positive outlook as essential to well being and have suggested that one gets or finds whatever one looks for in any given situation. Resources are therefore available to everyone who wishes to "improve" their outlooks on life.

Flowing with necessary changes is much easier, though not always a breeze, if one knows how adjustment to change takes place. My own interest in adjustment to change dates back to my graduate school days in the 1960s. Over the years, my own research and my reading of other people's investigations has convinced me that there is a natural, predictable sequence of stages that one's adjustment to change passes through. If one knows what is needed in each of these stages, one can adjust and get "back to normal" with less emotional and physical cost. When we are experiencing the tougher periods of change adjustment, it is much easier to be patient and "trust the process" if we "know" that brighter days and broader opportunities lie ahead!

In *Life Changes* (Spencer and Adams, 1990), we proposed that there are seven stages in transition adjustment — although each person is unique and therefore it's possible that some people might not experience every stage or may not progress through the stages in exactly the same manner as another person.

How acutely one experiences these seven stages of adjustment is a strongly influenced by several factors including: 1. Novelty (degree of surprise and unfamiliarity), 2. Clarity of expectations, 3. Number of other changes being experienced, 4. Life stage (e.g. during mid-life, seemingly small stages are sometimes experienced as being highly stressful), and 5. Personality (some people are more inclined to explore the emotional dimensions of their experiences than are others). The seven stages are portrayed in Figure 11 and are described briefly.

Stage one: Losing Focus. In the first few hours after one becomes aware that they have entered into a significant change (e.g. the announcement that your job has been abolished or just after your first marriage ceremony), there is likely to be a period of being unable to concentrate or make sense of what is going on around us. Our "circuits" have quickly overloaded, making it difficult for us to plan or stay focused. This brief stage is sometimes called "The shocking fuzzies."

Stage two: Minimization. As the change settles in for a few hours, it is normal that we will try to rationalize away its impact through minimizing or trivializing the change. This stage, also sometimes referred to as "the dance of denial" may last for a few hours or a few months depending on how "big" the change is.

Stage three: The Pit. Eventually, our attempts to deny the reality of

Figure 11 — The Seven Stages of
Transition and Adjustment

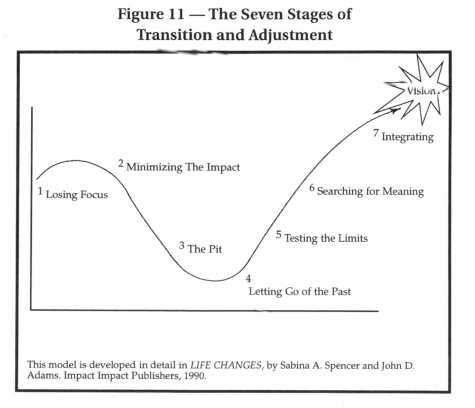

Vision

7 Integrating

2 Minimizing The Impact

1 Losing Focus

6 Searching for Meaning

3 The Pit

5 Testing the Limits

4
Letting Go of the Past

This model is developed in detail in *LIFE CHANGES*, by Sabina A. Spencer and John D. Adams. Impact Impact Publishers, 1990.

the change and the adjustment required give way to the awareness that "This is for real," and that the full adjustment is going to take some time. It is during this stage that we are likely to experience strong feelings of remorse, fear or anger over whatever it is that we have been required to let go of. This is the most stressful stage of the adjustment process, and we often compound it for ourselves by forgetting to look after ourselves (i.e. giving up any good habits we have as reflected in the **Self Management** section above). We are also most likely, while we are in the pit, to withdraw from our friends and supporters, the very people who could nurture us through the "storm."

Stage four: Letting Go. Most people eventually are able to turn around and shift their focus from the past and the pain of the present to the opportunities of the future. This stage, also called "the breakthrough," can happen suddenly and unexpectedly. It is also often aided by a self-created ritual or ceremony or by a "surprise" success experience.

Stage five: Testing. The testing stage is usually a more active and outwardly focused stage of adjustment, in which we try out the "new" state as it emerges or clarifies. We are likely to seek out and even sometimes exceed the limits during this more positive period of adjustment.

Stage six: Seeking Meaning. This is also called the "Treasure Hunting" stage of the adjustment process. It is a period of gradually lessening activity and increasing attention to what we have learned from the whole experience. Many feel the need to "give something back" during this stage — it is the people in this stage who keep the various support groups, like weight watchers and AA, alive and energized, and seek opportunities to serve as mentors and guides to others who are earlier on the adjustment "path."

Stage seven: Integration. And, at last, we arrive at the stage in which whatever we have learned from the adaptation is fully integrated and we no longer think much about it.

3. HABIT MANAGEMENT: Whenever there are changes taking place, habit patterns are disrupted, causing additional pressures and diverting attention away from productive effort. So, the question becomes "How does one make habit changes that stay changed?" I found in a recent study that at least four qualities are seemingly necessary for successful (i.e. self-sustaining) habit changes, whether the habits are personal or shared (as in "corporate cultures"): **passionate commitment, mechanisms that require repetitions, a goal and a few action steps**, and **solid support**.

In my study, I invited a number of people to tell me stories about times when they had set out to change major habits or fundamental patterns in their lives. I recorded their stories and asked only questions of clarification. The stories I heard were rich and detailed, as people seemed universally eager to share their successes. I felt both humble and honored by the openness and depth of the sharing I encountered. The stories were also quite varied, including decisions to adopt a spiritual path, to sever relationships with parents and siblings; to undertake major career shifts; to publicly adopt a new sexual preference; to change inner beliefs about father figures and authorities; and to reframe the true "meaning of life."

After I had collected several dozen such stories, I worked with the raw transcripts to seek those qualities that were most often present in the stories. I was absolutely amazed that all of the above four qualities were present in *over 90%* of the stories! Three additional qualities were present in over 70% of the success stories: *integrity* with personal values (i.e. if the person could see how making the change supported her or his values, it was easier to maintain the necessary level of commitment); *faith* in spiritual guidance or in "trusting the process;" and the existence of an external *"wake up call."* It appeared that in those cases in which there was no external wake up call or requirement (e.g. losing one's job in a down sizing activity), exceptional levels of internally driven commitment and a very strong external support system were necessary for success.

The importance of **integrity** to maintaining personal balance in a changing world is dealt with below, in the section called **Life Management. Trusting the Process** was mentioned in the previous section on **Novelty Management** as an essential to **flowing** with the unfolding of any given change.

Passionate commitment means that the person has truly made the intended change a priority over a long period of time. It takes a lot of "repetitions" for a new habit to replace an old "comfortable" one. Without sufficient commitment to following through, we often give up before we have engaged in enough repetitions of the new behavior to get it "into place." Those who made the change their enduring number one priority had the best successes in making habit changes.

Since the "autopilot" nature of our habit patterns always operates to reassert the former state and to resist the new, discipline is necessary in order to make the specified change successfully. In my research, this discipline usually took the form of **mechanisms or structures**, such as scheduled "rehearsals" of the new, and other such processes which require the new patterns to be used. Without this dedication to being successful, the autopilot often wins, and the habit change doesn't occur. It appears that whenever a deep change is undertaken, one needs to formally schedule "practices" of the new into one's life to reduce the autopilot nature of the outgoing habit and build up a "bank account" for the new one.

Third, a **goal and a few action steps** were clearly present in virtually every successful habit change. I was a little surprised that no one in my study ever mentioned "planning," but almost everyone had a clear goal, vision or outcome in mind. And almost everyone had a few first steps in mind. It seems that with a goal and a few steps, the appropriate succeeding steps make themselves clear. In the absence of "knowing clearly what I want," backsliding is easier.

Solid support also is necessary for making a transition from any significant habit pattern to a new one. Without such support, which might include both tangible and intangible rewards, as well as encouragement, direct assistance, expertise, challenge, and leadership, it is terribly easy to slide back to the old habit patterns. This might take the form of a person or small group one can turn to for encouragement and emotional support when the going gets tough, or a personal spiritual process, or even a pet cat to tell one's troubles to. Different people have widely differing needs for support and sources for finding that support. What became clear in investigating the success stories was that *some* kind of unquestioned support was almost universally present!

I also asked a number of people to tell me stories of times when they set out to make significant pattern changes in their lives and failed to follow through. Just as the above qualities were almost always present in the success stories, they were all noticeably absent in the failure stories! These four qualities may not be everything that is needed for successful habit pattern changes, but they certainly seem to be among the essentials!

4. PERFORMANCE MANAGEMENT: In addition to health management, novelty management, and habit management, we are often called upon (or choose internally) to protect and promote our capacities to perform at high levels in our work or other activities. There is some evidence that such optimal performance levels can contribute to enhancing our overall sense of well being during periods of rapid change. As Figure 12 portrays, both too little and too much pressure lead to diminished performance. If one can learn to monitor the level of pressure and take appropriate actions, they can keep themselves more of the time in the optimal zone.

As suggested earlier in this chapter, the Strain Response questionnaire can be helpful in noting when one is being pushed outside the optimal zone. For most people, simply noting an increased frequency of sighing is sufficient to conclude that one has moved away from the zone of optimal performance. But a further question remains. Even if a person manages her pressure level to remain within the optimal performance zone, she may *not* perform up to the top of the curve. Some additional qualities are necessary.

The four most fundamental components of such a climate, in my experience are an appropriate level of **challenge,** a balance of system **control** and freedom, a high degree of personal **commitment,** and as much **clarity** as can be provided about direction, responsibilities, standards, and so on. When these four "C's" are present, people are able to sustain high levels of performance without burning out.

LIFE MANAGEMENT: In Chapter Eight, I described a research investigation into the strongest determinants of happiness and fulfillment. The findings of that investigation were that these desirable life qualities were most influenced by meaningful work, the ability to use one's lifelong talents in meaningful ways, and good quality relationships both at work and away from work. So, two of the core competencies in the Life Management area are **Meaning** and **Relationships.**

Figure 12 — The Relationships Among Pressure, Performance and Health

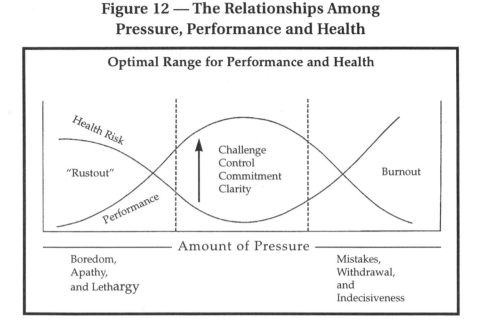

I find it significant that when I ask people to quickly brainstorm what has the most value and **meaning** in their lives, they usually speak first about health, then about family, and third about doing work that is of use to someone. When I ask the same people to identify how they actually focus their time and attention, the order is reversed — first priority goes to work, whether or not it has real meaning, then to relationships with family and friends, and finally, if there is time and energy, to their own health. Is it any wonder, then, that so many of us feel that we are out of balance most of the time and always racing to catch up with ourselves?

In addition to the finding that our relationships are predictors of our sense of life satisfaction, it has long been known that the quality of our **relationships** is a predictor of the quality of our health. John Cassell (1976), for example, found that the quality of support a person experiences is a strong predictor of both health and life expectancy. His conclusions have been supported in a number of studies involving both employment and away from employment focuses.

In the section above on Habit Management, I mentioned that **integrity** with values and personal sense of purpose is an essential quality for making successful habit pattern changes. When someone is able to align a desirable change with one of his or her central values or sense of life purpose, it is much easier for that person to generate the commitment needed to follow through successfully on the intended change. It has been my observation in over twenty years of working with health and stress management that those who live lives of integrity fare much better in their overall level of health than do those who can't seem to practice what they preach.

Versatility has been a favorite word of mine for at least twenty years. Unfortunately, it has not gotten enough visibility to be in general usage. By "versatility" I mean "appropriate flexibility." Most people have heard the adage that if the only tool you have is a hammer, then everything around you becomes a nail. If one is rigidly focused on meeting deadlines, one will be busy and get lots of results, but accuracy, teamwork and overall vision may suffer. If one is rigidly focused on accuracy, then results, teamwork and vision may suffer. And so on. It should be pretty obvious that the most effective people in the long run are likely to be those who are able to focus on results when results are called for, accuracy when accuracy is called for, teamwork when teamwork is called for, and vision when vision is called for. Behavioral versatility, as well as the mental versatility described in the previous chapter, contributes to overall high level performance in ways that actually prevent burnout. Low versatility of behavior and thinking limits effectiveness to narrow "bands" and actually hastens burnout.

As the complexities and challenges around us continue to grow, surely meaning, relationships, integrity and versatility will only increase in their importance to our living full and balanced lives.

To summarize this chapter reminding us of the essential immediate responses to a rapidly changing world, it is important that we create workplace and home activities which:

✦ encourage good stress protection and health promotion habits such as **breathing, regular exercise, regular relaxation, and balanced diet;**

✧ provide excellent novelty management capabilities such as **information, skills, positive attitude, ability to flow;**

✧ support ourselves in changing individual and team habit patterns through **commitment, discipline, goal/first steps, and support;**

✧ create a sustainable high performance work environment characterized by **challenge, control, commitment and clarity;**

✧ foster satisfying and fulfilling personal experiences through **meaning, relationships, integrity, and versatility.**

Questions For Contemplation And Dialogue

✧ Why am I working so hard these days — in order to do what?

✧ When will it be okay to NOT work fourteen-hour days in my company?

✧ Is the work we are now doing going to get us to where we want to be in thirty years?

✧ What do I (we) wish to be remembered for?

✧ Many people like me are making career shifts — what can we do to make a bigger difference?

✧ How can I better use my current awareness to guide my actions to build a legacy of hope, equality, peace, well being, harmony, and a clean environment?

✧ How can I make myself available beyond the boundaries of my job?

✧ How do I move from fear to action?

✧ How can I connect my present work with the emerging global challenges?

✧ How can I "rediscover" my children, so that their future will have meaning?

✧ Can we influence our organizations to reinvest in families?

TEN

Thinking Today As If Tomorrow Mattered

～

"That person who lives completely free from desires without longing attains peace."

BHAGAVAD GITA

"He who knows he has enough is rich."

TAO TE CHING

"Whoever in the world overcomes his selfish cravings, his sorrows shall fall away from him, like drops of water from a flower."

DHAMMAPADA

"We have modified our environment so radically, we must now modify ourselves in order to exist in this new environment.

NORBERT WEINER

Past As Prologue

Let us begin this final chapter with a statement from the past that is as alive with meaning today as it was nearly 150 years ago. Many of the Native American tribes felt a oneness with the Earth and with all of the species that lived on the Earth. In general, they felt that all must live in harmony, and that no species was more special or more entitled than any other. In this sense, the Native Americans were practicing systems thinking long before it gained academic respectability across the "developed" world.

One of the most incredible expressions of the Native Americans' sense of interrelationships of all living beings and the Earth is contained in a letter from Chief Seattle to U.S. President Franklin Pierce, in response to the U.S. attempt to buy the land inhabited by Chief Seattle's people. Although the original has been lost, the following translation is often quoted:

> How can you buy or sell the sky? The land? This idea is strange to us. If we do not own the freshness of the air and the sparkle of the water, how can you buy them? Every aspect of this Earth is sacred to my people. Every shining pine needle, every sandy shore, every mist in the dark woods, every meadow, every humming insect. All are holy in the memory and experience of my people.
>
> If we sell you "our" land, remember that the air is precious to us, that the air shares its spirit with all the life it supports. The wind that gave our grandfather his first breath also received his last sigh. The wind also gives our children the spirit of life. So, if we sell you "our" land, you must keep it apart and sacred, as a place where man can go to taste the wind that is sweetened by the meadow flowers.
>
> Will you teach your children what we have taught our

children? That the Earth is our mother? Whatever befalls the Earth befalls all the children of the Earth.

This we know: the Earth does NOT belong to man; man belongs to the Earth. All things are connected like the blood that unites us all. Man did NOT weave the web of life, he is merely a strand within it. Whatever man does to the web of life he does to himself.

One thing we know: our God is your God. The Earth is precious to Him and to harm the Earth is to heap contempt on its creator.

I'll See It When I Believe It

As I suggested at the outset of this book, there are many who would argue that there is nothing to be concerned about, that all of the foregoing is a silly exercise. Others will say that the writing here doesn't go far enough to outline the critical nature of the situation. How we hold the future depends on our prevailing perspectives. If I hold a belief strongly, I will tend to find evidence to support my position and to counter opposing positions. History tells us that it is highly unlikely that we will be swayed by the arguments of those who hold different opinions from ours, and that it is equally unlikely that we will sway them to our point of view.

There have been many highly vigorous debates between those who hold that there is nothing to worry about relative to a sustainable future and those who are convinced that we must take drastic actions very soon in order to have any future at all. Consider the following points of view.[9]

1. Julian L. Simon, University of Maryland:

The proposition that there is a crisis in our environment is all wrong on the scientific facts . . . The U.S. EPA makes

---

[9] From "The Global Environment: Megaproblem or Not?" *The Futurist*. March-April, 1997, pp 17-22.

clear that our air and water have been getting cleaner . . .
Every agricultural economist knows that the world has
been eating better on average since WWII . . . Every
resource economist knows that natural resources are
becoming more available rather than more scarce . . .
Every demographer knows that the death rate has been
falling all over the world . . . It is also clear that population
growth does NOT hinder economic development.

2. Ronald Bailey, Competitive Enterprise Institute.

Food is more abundant and cheaper than it has ever been
. . .Economic growth leads to less pollution, not more . . .
Greater knowledge and wealth enable us to respond flex-
ibly and effectively to the unexpected . . . History shows
that the best way to avoid the "tragedy of the commons"
is through ownership. . . History shows that private ownership, whether individuals or groups, commercial or
noncommercial, offers the best defense against environmental degradation . . . Simply by protecting their prop-
erty, individual owners incidentally protect the earth for
the rest of us.

3. Hazel Henderson, Independent Futurist.

Individual per capita averages do not tell you how the
poverty gap is widening, or how much of this food, even
at lower prices, is available to people who don't have ANY
money . . . There are 1.6 billion people in the world who
are worse off than they were fifteen years ago . . . Thirty
years ago there was a 30 to 1 difference between the richest 20% and the poorest 20% of humanity; now it is 60 to
1 . . . Prices do not include environmental and social costs
. . . Economists think that by increasing the rapidity of the
exploitation of resources, somehow the inflating money
balance sheet will constantly produce more money to
"clean up the problem."

4. Dennis Pirages, University of Maryland.

> First there's the time baseline - if one goes back to the Neanderthals as a baseline, it's not difficult to find signs of progress. If one starts in 1980, it's a little more difficult . . . It's not possible to diffuse the West's materially comfortable lifestyle to the entire planet without destroying the environment . . . Our goal should be to create a more sustainable society - through our values and institutions, policies and technologies, systems and paradigms . . . The accounting methods we now use pay little attention to intangibles like climatic stability, biological diversity, unspoiled landscapes, clean air and water, and a melanoma free day at the beach.

Is it likely that Simon and Bailey changed their minds after hearing from Henderson and Pirages? I think not! Is it likely that anyone in attendance at this debate or anyone reading this book has changed their viewpoints as a result of the arguments advanced by one or more of these speakers? Of course not! If anything, arguments such as these serve only to reinforce the viewpoints people already hold and increase the polarization from those who hold differing viewpoints.

So who is right? Paradoxically, all four are correct in their arguments. Will debates such as these lead to any constructive outcomes? Unlikely.

Current Reality

In 1992, approximately 10,000 diplomats and business leaders from nearly 180 nations met in Rio for an Earth Summit to work towards cleaning up the planet. The work at the Earth Summit, and the agreements reached, received broad coverage in world-wide media. Five years later, in 1997, the summit was assessed by a "Rio Plus Five" forum, and the results were disappointing. According to Maurice Strong, the Canadian industrialist who was Secretary General of the Earth Summit,

"Overall, we haven't made a fundamental course of
change promised in Rio in 1992. We have won some bat-
tles, but we are losing the war. Five years later, the challenge is even grerater."[10]

In 1992, 153 nations signed treaties to prevent global warming, save
endangered species, and promote a sustainable form of economic
development. The review by the Rio Plus Five forum learned that millions of acres of rain forests, wetlands, and coral reefs are still being
destroyed each year, that our water and air are more polluted than
they were in 1992, and that the world is supporting an additional half
billion people.

Former U.S. congresswoman and former President of the Women's
Environment and Development Organization, Bella Abzug, summed
the situation up as follows:

"We get all these terrific, conscientious agreements, and
then we go home and they (governments) don't do anything about them."[11]

Only five countries, for example, are expected to reach the treaty's
goals for the year 2000 for global warming gas emissions. And the
decrease in the emissions of three of these five, Russia, Poland and the
Czech Republic, is not due to policy changes, but to the closure of anti-
quated factories after the fall of the Berlin Wall!

While some progress has been made since the Rio Earth Summit,
and people around the world are now more educated about the
importance of the environment, not one country has reached full
compliance with the 1992 agreements.

The Worldwatch Institute recently reported that world fishery production has leveled off and begun to decline, and that world grain production has declined dramatically and annually since 1984.

In the area of wealth distribution, the disparity between rich and

---

[10] *San Francisco Chronicle.* March 20, 1997, pg. A10.
[11] Ibid

poor has also gotten much larger in the past five years. In 1992, the average large company CEO was annually making about 157 times as much as the lowest paid workers in the same company. By 1997, this gap had risen to just over 200 to 1.

These are the conditions that are concerning many people around the world. As the experts continue to debate with each other, as illustrated above, conditions continue to deteriorate. Let us recall again the metaphor introduced by Karl-Henrik Robèrt in Chapter 4, about the monkeys chattering at each other up in the branches of a tree about the loss of leaves, while the tree is sick in its roots, out of sight of all the chattering.

Is That a Light At the End of the Tunnel Or The Headlight of a Speeding Train?

Futurist Willis Harman (*Global Mind Change*, 1990) used to point out frequently in his speeches that whenever anxiety increases, people can be expected to react in more extreme ways. For example, conservatives become more conservative, and liberals become more liberal. While this assertion is not ALWAYS true, it is USUALLY true, in my experience. We can perhaps understand this more clearly by looking at the triangle in Figure 13.

If we oversimplify the way people think by suggesting three different points of view, each one of us could be "located" somewhere in the triangle to depict our balance of viewpoints. Thus, someone who generally feels that we should take responsibility for the future and protect the planet for future generations might be located at position "1" in the triangle, relatively near to the RESPONSIBILITY corner of the triangle. And someone who generally feels that "the one who dies with the most toys wins" might be located at position "2" in the triangle, relatively near the ENTITLEMENT corner. Someone who generally feels that trusting a higher power to take care of things is the best thing to do might be located at position "3" in the triangle, relatively nearer to the TRANSCENDENT corner.

Figure 13 — Predominant World Views

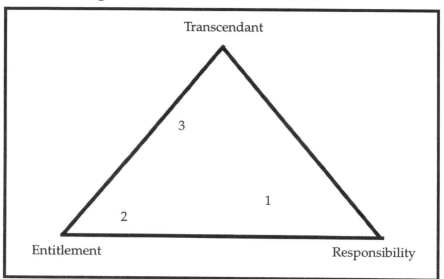

Let's assume that the pressure builds up to high levels on the society, to the point that some people begin to act out of extreme positions. For example, as the pressure builds, we might expect some of the people at position "1" to move closer to that corner, perhaps becoming a radical environmentalists. Likewise, some of the people at position "2" would move closer to that corner, perhaps joining an ultra right wing militia group. And some of the people at position "3" would likely move to a retreat center or ashram, or join a new age cult that expects to transcend to another reality any day now...

I believe that we are seeing this phenomena happen across our society today. As environmentalist groups become stronger and more vocal, so too do militia groups and newly evolving spiritual movements. Behavior patterns seem to be polarizing and becoming more extreme in every walk of life, making true dialogue and an integrated community seem impossible.

While this may seem frightening or at least disheartening, I think that it also contains the seeds of a successful way ahead. Out of the ferment of the present day debates between liberal and conservative, between Left and Right, a new consciousness has been identified that holds different outlooks and different values. As we are so often reminded by the words of Albert Einstein, we can't expect to resolve a challenge from within the same consciousness that created it in the first place.

There is no doubt that the Left and the Right are equally committed to actions that are unsustainable, for neither side espouses anything approaching the kind of actions necessary for a sustainable presence, as outlined in Chapter 4 by Karl-Henrik Robèrt. However, arising from the dialectic of their on-going debates seems to be a new way of thinking and a new way of being on the planet.

Paul Ray (1996) has spent several years conducting research on the values, lifestyles, and worldviews of Americans. Ray's conclusion is that we are living during a period in which our culture (and by implication, the cultures of many people around the world) is changing very rapidly — much more rapidly than most of us are aware of. This can be highly disorienting and fraught with conflicts whose roots are only dimly, at best, understood by most people. Ray sees nothing short of the appearance of a new cultural form which is emerging very rapidly, at least across the United States.

Ray receives support in this idea from Ken Wilber (1996), in his book *A Brief History of Everything*:

> The rational-industrial (modern) worldview, having served its purposes, is now living on its own fumes. We are breathing our own exhaust. And how we handle this, how we collectively handle this, will determine whether a new and more adequate worldview emerges to defuse these problems, or whether we are buried in our own wastes...This extraordinary modern flower blossomed in its glorious spring, and now can do nothing but watch its own leaves fall dead on the ground of a rising tomorrow. (P. 68)

Paul Ray refers to the people who make up the two largest subcultures as "Heartlanders" — holders of traditional values and viewpoints, and "Modernists" — holders of the "official" establishment viewpoints and values. Emerging rapidly are the "Cultural Creatives," so named because they are in a process of creating a whole new cultural tradition in which Left and Right, liberal and conservative are meaningless designations.

In Ray's view, this emergence of a new subculture has happened only once or twice a millennium over the last 3500 years, and that, following a period of turbulence and chaos, a new dominant culture sends humanity in altogether new directions. While this can obviously be highly unsettling to us today, especially those of us who are benefiting greatly from the presently dominating system of financial growth and success, it can also herald the dawning of a new approach to the challenges this book has been addressing. Rather than trying to figure out how to resolve the present challenges, it may be better to find ways to stimulate the growth of this new set of values and world views! To quote Ray:

> Take heart! Unbeknownst to most of us, we're traveling in the midst of an enormous company of allies: a larger population of creative people, who are the carriers of more positive ideas, values and trends than any previous Renaissance Period has ever seen. And, they can probably be mobilized to act altruistically on behalf of our future. (Ray, 1996, p 3).

Ray calls today's dominant subculture the "Moderns." The Moderns make up 47% of the U.S. population today, and of the three subcultures, have the highest mean incomes and the highest percentage of professionals and business people. 54% are male, and 46% are female. While none of the subcultures holds monolithic world views or values, each can be characterized by those values and outlooks which they hold most strongly or most frequently across the subculture.

Moderns are most likely of the three subcultures to:

⋄ Focus on status and success.

⋄ Hold materialistic values, emphasizing upward mobility.

⋄ Be most cynical about politics.

⋄ Not be self actualizing.

⋄ Not be altruistic.

⋄ Be opposed to environmental sustainability initiatives.

⋄ Hold a world view based on day to day concerns.

⋄ Hold a "more of the same" image of the future.

⋄ Be most pessimistic about the future.

The second largest subculture identified by Ray is the "Heartlanders," who make up 29% of the U.S. population. Of the three subcultures, the Heartlanders are relatively the oldest, have the lowest mean income and educational levels, and the lowest percentage of business and professional people and the highest percentage of retired people. 46% of Heartlanders are male, and 54% are female.

As a group, Heartlanders are most likely of the three subcultures to:

⋄ Be religious conservatives, to join the "religious right."

⋄ Favor traditional relationships, to be family centered.

⋄ Be against feminism.

⋄ Be intolerant of diversity, be Xenophobic.

⋄ Have low regard for civil rights.

⋄ Hold a world view based on nostalgia and myths about the past.

⋄ Long for simple solutions.

⋄ Hold an "idealized past" as their image of the future.

The third large subculture identified by Ray, the "Cultural Creatives," were too few to be measured in previous research on values, and has emerged very rapidly since the 1960s. Cultural Creatives currently make up at least 24% of the U.S. population. Only 40% are male, while 60% are female. Of the three subcultures, Cultural Creatives have the highest average levels of education.

As a group, the Cultural Creatives are most likely to:

◈ Hold global viewpoints, be Xenophiles.

◈ Be supportive of ecological sustainability initiatives, hold "green" values.

◈ Be less compelled towards material success.

◈ Be supportive of feminism.

◈ Hold a world view based on ideals and on new views of humanity.

◈ Be interested in developing a new image of the future.

◈ Be most optimistic about the future.

In the Post World War II years, the Heartlanders and the Moderns each comprised about half of the U.S. population. Since the 60's though, the Heartlanders have diminished dramatically (now about 29%) and the Cultural Creatives have emerged rapidly (now about 24%), leaving the Moderns (47%) as the dominant subculture in our society. As we have seen in the previous chapters, this domination has presided over a *dis-integration* of our society — with the rich getting rapidly richer, the poor getting poorer; human activity being strongly seen as being separate from nature; brilliant technological breakthroughs that two thirds of the global population has no access to; and growing strife and conflict among the "outsiders" (i.e. the non-Moderns and the less affluent).

In this book, I have been somewhat arbitrarily considering the end of the 20th Century to be a major turning point in Human history. How will historians regard it? As a passing storm leading to a bright new day; or as a period of turbulence preceding steady decline into chaos and despair? The opportunities are unparalleled in human history — but there is no guarantee of a golden age of prosperity, as the Post Moderns may shake our culture to pieces. The challenges, too, are unparalleled in human history — but sliding into a morass is not inevitable — as a growing segment of the population is poised (although "it" doesn't realize this yet) to trigger a renaissance.

One thing we cannot have much longer is "more of the same," as few of the present trends outlined in this book are sustainable over the long term.

The qualities of our dominant images of the future, and the qualities of the efforts based on them will create whatever future we do have. As we know very well, our outlooks and world views tend to be self fulfilling, and a lot depends on how optimistic or pessimistic our predominant future view is. In *The Image of the Future*, Fred Polak (1973) found that pessimistic societies historically have deteriorated rather quickly.

As mentioned, the Cultural Creatives have emerged, largely unnoticed, since the 60's. Their "spirit" is fueled by the desire to heal the splits they experience in society — between the inner and the outer; between the material and the spiritual; and between the individual and society. Perhaps the briefest way to summarize how the Cultural Creative way of thinking is different is that it tends to be characterized by a "feminine whole systems" point of view.

Thus, if their numbers do continue to grow to the point where they become the dominant thinking force in society, the emerging new society will come to be characterized by *reintegration*. An early example is the already emerging reintegration of science and spirituality, creating what has come to be called "the new science."

With Cultural Creatives as the dominant thinking style, we might expect an emergent society in which ecological sustainability was a business priority; in which psychology and spirituality merged; in which there was a blending and balancing of masculine and feminine energies; and in which a social consciousness of the oneness of all was taught from earliest years at school. We would have a whole new genre of media and literature. The Internet would be alive with new ideas for community. Different, far less material, purchasing patterns would emerge. Interest in self-development would skyrocket, as would awareness of good nutrition and the prevention of illness. These emerging qualities are already quite visible to anyone who cares to look.

The Challenge of Networking

The present challenge is in getting the Cultural Creatives together, for there are already sufficient numbers to have a huge impact on the mainstream ways of thinking. Being by nature somewhat insular and withdrawn from the mainstream that they resist, the Cultural Creatives by and large have no idea about how many similarly minded people there are around them (24% of the U.S. population and growing rapidly).

There are plenty of indications, as well, that the Cultural Creative mindset is emerging everywhere around the world. All that is needed are mechanisms for bringing them together in dialogue, to find ways to envision the future collectively and begin to put it into place. We don't need to put huge amounts of energy into debating with people who *disagree* with us; rather we should be dialoguing with those who *agree* with us!

I do not in any way mean to suggest that present efforts to protect and clean up the environment should cease. Nor do I want those who are concerned about the global economy and those who are concerned about the growth of the global population to cease their work. What I do mean to suggest is that these activities, being rooted in the same consciousness that has created the challenges in the first place, will not, in and of themselves, be sufficient to establish a sustainable human presence on the planet. In addition to these noble causes, I am calling for overt and significant efforts among those who identify with the Cultural Creative qualities to create networks that engage in "like-minded" dialogue.

Through the process of dialogue, people can deepen their understanding of their core beliefs and values, and through such engagement, the emergence of a new consciousness is likely; a consciousness which can and will successfully engage with the challenges to sustainability. Thus, the ultimate issue is not sustainable business practices or sustainable environmental laws, but rather *sustainable consciousness*.

It is well known that established systems, be they individual, group, organizational, societal, or global, have an inherent tendency to resist change. We resist the unfamiliar and the unknown, even when we know that the change will be good for us. In Western culture, the usual response to resistance is to confront it head-on, polarizing those who want to change and those who are resistant; then others, who may have been less resistant initially join the confrontation on the side of those who are perceived to be under "attack." Ultimately, the more powerful elements of the system force the change into place, and a sizable number of system members are left bruised (or worse) and alienated. Networking offers an effective alternative; an alternative that is naturally attractive to the "feminine-whole system" thinking of the Cultural Creatives.

Networking To Generate New Thinking

Networks of people are operating every day in all kinds of settings. We all have contacts we can go to, to get things done when the "system" is moving too slowly. People use support networks to resolve situations and recover from addictions. Most of us have people we turn to (or can) for emotional support, advice, energizing, respect, or intimacy. Networks can also help to bring about change if we use them to follow the path of least resistance.

One of the founders of the field of organizational behavior, Herbert Shepard, used to point out "If you want to create change, don't work uphill if you don't have to — and don't build hills for yourself as you go along." If we take this advice and couple it with the collective wisdom of those who work with implementing planned changes in organizations, we have the networking model for generating change illustrated in Figure 14.

Whenever a new idea is introduced, approximately equal numbers of people (10-15%) can be expected to be strongly supportive and vehemently resistant. Further, approximately equal numbers are likely to be "early adopters" of the idea and "late adopters" in relation to the idea (30-40%). For almost any new idea, the affected population

Figure 14 — Networking Model of Change

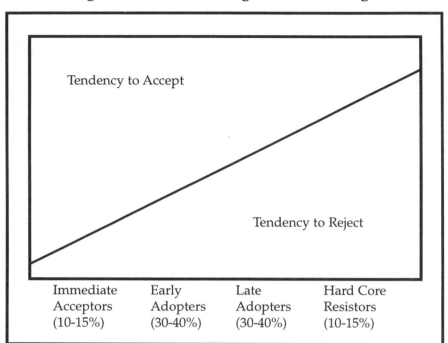

Tendency to Accept

Tendency to Reject

| Immediate Acceptors (10-15%) | Early Adopters (30-40%) | Late Adopters (30-40%) | Hard Core Resistors (10-15%) |

will respond in these four ways. However, it should also be pointed out that an immediate acceptor of one idea may be a hard core resistor of a different proposed change.

We will be more successful in generating changes (and in catalyzing new consciousness!) if we begin by identifying the strong supporters of the idea and helping them to network with each other. People's jobs, socio-economic status, and so on are irrelevant in a network of avid supporters. They identify with each other because they have a common vision rather than giving much attention to their status in other realms of their lives.

The next steps are to bring the Immediate Acceptors together and to draw upon their creativity and mutual interest in planning how to approach the Early Adopters without alienating the Hard Core Resistors. Rather, the Late Adopters and the Hard Core Resistors should be encouraged to keep open minds, and to speak their minds as well, for the sharing from those who disagree helps in uncovering "issues" that might otherwise be overlooked. As the Early Adopters begin to "sing along with the choir," they can help with ideas for bringing along the Late Adopters. In this way, a critical mass of supporters of the new idea is established with relative ease.

While this description is brief and general, the principle of networking among the strongest supporters of a new idea has proven to be a very powerful one in implementing change. In fact, informal networks of people have almost always been behind major social changes. The established or dominant system can be expected to perpetuate itself, whether that system be a local club, a charity organization or the dominant mode of thinking across a culture. Few, if any, systems have ever chosen voluntarily to undergo radical change or to end their existence. Major change, therefore, has usually been "driven" by nonsanctioned networks of dedicated people.

For example, George Washington and his "network" of underground rebels struggled against the established order of George III of England to create a new order of things now referred to as the United States. Ironically, this "new order" now labels contemporary networks seeking to make major social changes as enemies.

The lesson to be remembered is simple: *It is difficult or impossible to make fundamental change in the basic context or "reality" of any given system when operating from within that context or reality.* Fundamental changes can occur only when a critical mass (25-30%?) of people are able to see, accept, and commit to another "reality."

There are many enquiry and dialogue processes available today. To name just a few, Peter Senge (1990) has been working actively with dialogue groups through his center at MIT for a number of years. Juanita Brown and David Isaacs have long based their corporate consulting work on the establishment of "Good Conversation." Brown's latest innovation in the area of dialogue is called "The World Café" (www.theworldcafe.com). Doug Engelbart (www.bootstrap.org), who was the inventor of the computer "mouse" and many other innovations that make today's PC world possible, now supports and enhances the work of "Networked Improvement Communities" (NICs) through his organization, The Bootstrap Institute. Prof. David Cooperrider, at Case-Western Reserve University, has pioneered a unique enquiry process called "Appreciative Enquiry." These are just a few of the many networking and dialoguing resources that have sprung up during the 1990's.

To get a clearer picture of how this networking process promotes change, we need to briefly review the characteristics of "declining" and "emerging" cultures (Capra, 1982). The apparent declining culture (or paradigm) is the mechanistic mindset of the Moderns. It is rooted in the thinking of the 17th Century. Galileo, Descartes, Bacon and Newton fostered a New World view that, in its time, fostered a revolution in consciousness. Descartes viewed the universe as a machine. He believed that mechanical laws could account for everything beyond the realm of the soul. This ultimately led to a reductionist approach to the sciences, in which everything was to be broken down into its smallest parts, just as a machine can be disassembled into its component parts.

All scientific disciplines subsequently adopted the mechanistic (modern) paradigm. This new way of thinking resulted in tremendous advances in both theory and technology for over 350 years. It has also contributed to today's growing list of seemingly insurmountable global challenges.

Perhaps the mechanistic paradigm has reached the point of diminishing returns. The major successes of that paradigm — science and technology — have shrunk the world, bringing diverse elements together in complex interdependencies which can no longer be addressed properly by mechanistic/reductionist thinking. Today, the "whole" of our world is greater than the sum of its parts. The analogy of the machine no longer serves to describe adequately the interdependencies of the global economy, global ecological emergencies, inequitable distribution of wealth, and so on.

Although physicists began to abandon the mechanistic/reduction-ist paradigm in the 1920s, the rest of Western culture, for the most part, still follows it closely. Descartes' revolution against the dogmatism of the Middle Ages has developed into a new dogmatism.

The emerging new culture will not wholly reject the declining culture, but will engulf it in a "larger" perception of reality. Apples will still fall from trees, gears will continue to transform engine power into motion. Mechanistic solutions will continue to be appropriate for resolving many challenges. However, other challenges will require a more holistic, feminine, global, interdependent, spiritual worldview. Their fundamental interconnectedness must be appreciated. This can only happen as a whole systems approach supplants reductionist mind sets.

Obviously, no existing government or business is actively working to generate this broader new culture. But even so, its manifestations are becoming obvious. It is emerging because of networks of committed and concerned individuals around the world. As the Internet reaches the smallest villages in developing countries, we can expect these networks to reach to those places as well.

The fires of social transformation are almost always sparked by networks of dedicated people. The dialogues at the nodes of these networks are creating the future, and all the network members are co-creators. To close with more from Ken Wilber (1996):

> And, of course, this new and wonderful transformation, which everyone seems to be yearning for, will nevertheless bring its own recalcitrant problems and brutal limitations. It will defuse some of the problems of rational-industrialization, which is wonderful, but it will create and unleash its own severe difficulties. (P. 70)

Questions For Contemplation And Dialogue

✧ What is the role and contribution of spirit in the workplace?

✧ How soon will I have to make hard choices about whom to serve?

✧ Whom shall I partner with?

✧ If it's not too late too make a difference, what is the most important thing for me to do?

✧ What do I need to heal inside?

✧ How do I stay with "questions" in a world of answers?

✧ How do I move from having answers to staying with the questions?

✧ How shall I restructure my own questions for the broadest and deepest awareness?

✧ Am I able to maintain global consciousness in my daily activities?

✧ How can we establish a values base to guide our work?

✧ How can I increase my sense of wholeness on a daily basis?

✧ How can we help each other find deeper meanings in our lives?

✧ What are some small immediate steps I can take?

✧ How can I integrate sustainable consciousness with every activity I undertake?

✧ How can we operate in our line of work from a consistent systems perspective?

✧ How can we foster sustainable consciousness without inducing guilt?

✧ What are the key leverage points for fostering a more sustainable consciousness in our workplace?

✧ What is our ideal imagined world? Can this vision guide our daily actions?

✧ What can we each do to maintain encouragement and persistence towards a sustainable consciousness?

✧ How can we support each other's passions for personal and social change?

✧ What can we do to influence our organizations to explore/dialogue about what really matters?

✧ What is it that pulls me away from that which matters most to me?

References and Further Reading

_____. *Business Week*, May 11, 1992, pp 65-75.

_____. *Business Week*, April 26, 1993, pp 56-79.

_____. *In Context: A Quarterly of Humane Sustainable Culture*. Bainbridge Island, WA.

_____. *World Business Academy Perspectives*. Burlingame, CA.

_____. *Business Strategy for Sustainable Development*. Winnipeg.

_____. *The Futurist*. Bethesda, MD: The World Future Society.

Adams, J., J. Hayes and B. Hopson. 1976. Transition: Understanding and Managing Personal Change. London: Martin Robertson & Company.

Adams, J. 1980. *"Improving Stress Management: An Action Research Based OD Intervention."* in W.W. Burke (Ed.). The Cutting Edge. San Diego, CA: University Associates.

Adams, J. 1998. *Transforming Work (2nd Ed.)*. Alexandria, VA: Miles River Press.

Adams, J. 1998. *Transforming Leadership (2nd Ed.)*. Alexandria, VA: Miles River Press.

Bailey, R. 1993. *Eco-Scam: The False Prophets of Ecological Apocalypse*. New York: St. Martin's.

Block, P. 1996. *Stewardship: Choosing Service Over Self Interest*. San Francisco: Berrett-Koehler.

Bolman, L. & T. Deal. 1995. *Leading With Soul*. San Francisco: Jossey-Bass.

Brown, L., C. Flavin & S. Postel. 1991. *Saving the Planet*. New York: W.W. Norton.

Capra, F. 1982. *The Turning Point*. New York: Simon & Schuster.

Cassell, John. 1976. "The Contribution of Social Environment to Host Resistance." *American Journal of Psychosomatic Research* 104 (2), pp 107-123.

Daly, H. E. & J. B. Cobb. 1991. *For the Common Good*. Boston: Beacon Press.

Douthwaite, R. 1992. *The Growth Illusion: How Economic Growth Has Enriched the Few, Impoverished the Many, And Endangered the Planet*. London: Resurgence.

Ehrlich, P.R., 1995. "The Equity Answer to the Human Dilemma." *The Commonwealth*. 89 (46), pp 1-7.

Ehrlich, P. R. & A. H. Ehrlich. 1991. *Healing the Planet*. Reading, MA: Addison-Wesley Pub. Co.

Enright, J. 1993. *In Our Face*. Menlo Park, CA: Intermedia.

Greco, Jr., T. H. 1992. *Money and Debt: A Solution to the Global Crisis*. Tucson, self-published.

Greco, Jr., T. H. 1994. *New Money For Healthy Communities*. Tucson: self-published.

Goldsmith, E. 1993. *The Way*. Boston: Shambala.

Gore, A. 1992. *Earth In The Balance*. New York: Houghton Mifflin Co.

Gribbin, J. (Ed). 1987. *The Breathing Planet*. New York: Basil Blackwell Inc.

Harman, W. 1990. *Global Mind Change*. New York: Warner Books.

Harman, W. 1992. *"Whatever Happened To Usury?"* WBA Perspectives, 6 (2).

Harman, W. 1994. *"A System In Decline or Transformation."* WBA Perspectives, 8 (2).

Harman, W. & J. Hormann. 1990. *Creative Work: The Constructive Role of Business In a Transforming Society*. Indianapolis: Knowledge Systems Inc.

Harman, W. & M. Porter. 1997. *The New Business of Business: Sharing Responsibility For a Positive Global Future*. San Francisco: Berrett-Koehler

Hawken, P. 1993. *The Ecology of Commerce*. New York: HarperBusiness.

Hawley, J. 1993. *Reawakening the Spirit In Work*. San Francisco: Berrett-Koehler.

Henderson, H. (1978). *Creating Alternative Futures*. New York: Putnam.

Henderson, H. (1988). *Politics of the Solar Age*. Indianapolis: Knowledge Systems Inc.

Henderson, H. (1991). *Paradigms in Progress*. Indianapolis: Knowledge Systems Inc.

Helmstetter, S. 1986. *What to Say When You Talk to Yourself*. New York: Pocket Books.

Hubbard, H.M., 1991 "The Real Cost of Energy." *Scientific American*, 264 (4), pp 36-42.

Korten, D. 1990. *Getting To the 21st Century*. West Hartford, CT: Kumarian Press.

Korten, D. 1995. *When Corporations Rule the World*. San Francisco: Berrett-Koehler.

Kurtzman, J. 1993. *The Death of Money: How the Electronic Economy Has Destabilized the World's Markets and Created Financial Chaos*. New York: Simon & Schuster.

Laing, R. 1990. In Zweig, C. And J. Abrams. *Meeting the Shadow*. Los Angeles: Jeremy P. Tarcher, Inc.

Mander, J. 1991. *In the Absence of the Sacred*. San Francisco: Sierra Club Books.

Meadows, D., D. Meadows, & J. Randers. 1992. *Beyond the Limits*. Post Mills, VT: Chelsea Green Publishing Company.

Minkin, B H. 1995. *Future in Sight*. New York: Macmillan.

Osterberg, R. 1993. *Corporate Renaissance*. Mill Valley, CA: Nataraj Publishing.

Ray, M. & A. Rinzler (Eds). 1993. *The New Paradigm in Business*. Los Angeles: Jeremy P. Tarcher.

Ray, P. 1996. *The Integral Culture Study*. Sausalito: Institute of Noetic Sciences.

Renesch, J. R. (Ed). 1992. *New Traditions in Business*. San Francisco: Berrett-Koehler.

Renesch, J. R. (Ed). 1994. *Leadership in a New Era: Visionary Approaches to the Biggest Crisis of Our Time*. San Francisco: New Leaders Press.

Renesch, J. & B. DeFoore. 1996. *The New Bottom Line: Bringing Heart and Soul to Business*. San Francisco: New Leaders Press.

Repeto, R. (1990) "Promoting Environmentally Sound Social Economic Progress: What the North Can Do." Washington, DC: World Resources Institute.

Rifkin, J. *The End of Work: The Decline of the Global Labor Force And the Dawn of the Post Market Era*. New York: Tarcher-Putnam.

Roszak, T. 1992. *The Voice of the Earth*. New York: Simon & Schuster.

Russell, P. 1992. *The White Hole in Time*. San Francisco: Harper/San Francisco.

Russell, P. 1995. *The Global Brain Awakens*. Menlo Park, CA: Global Brain Publications.

Schmidheiny, S. 1992. *Changing Course*. Cambridge, MA: MIT Press.

Schwartz, P. 1991. *The Art of the Long View*. New York: Currency Doubleday.

Schor, J. 1991. *The Overworked American: The Unexpected Decline of Leisure*. Bethesda, MD

Senge, P. 1990. *The Fifth Discipline*. New York: Currency Doubleday.

Simon, J.L. and H. L. Kahn. 1984. *The Resourceful Earth: A Response To the Global 2000 Report*. London: Basil Blackwell.

Spencer, S. and J. Adams. 1990. *Life Changes*. San Luis Obispo, CA: Impact Publishers.

Walter, David (Ed.). 1993. *Today Then: America's Best Minds Look Into the Future on the Occasion of the 1893 World's Columbian Exposition*. New York: American & World Geographic Publishing.

Wilber, K. (1996). *A Brief History of Everything*. Boston: Shambala Publications, Inc.

Willums, J.-O. & U. Goluke. 1992. *From Ideas to Action: Business and Sustainable Development*. New York: International Chamber of Commerce.

Order Information

You may order copies of *Thinking Today as if Tomorrow Mattered* directly from the author, for $14.95 plus $3.50 for shipping and handling per book. Individual orders must be prepaid, by check only. Checks should be made payable to *Eartheart Enterprises*. California residents add 8.5% sales tax.

Send your check to: John D. Adams
                      Eartheart Enterprises
                      1360 4th Avenue
                      San Francisco, CA 94122-2616

For discount orders (bookstores and individual orders over 20 books), please telephone 415-753-6668 for information. Large orders may be faxed to 415-753-6669.

You may also send enquiries about the book via e-mail to:
                      JohnDAdams@worldnet.att.net

Orders from outside the United States must be prepaid in U.S. funds, by a check payable through a U.S. branch of your local bank.